WHAT OTHERS ARE SAYING

If you are a Christian struggling with sin and failure, Leslie Smith's book, *Without Excuse*, is a must read. By reading her book, you will be pleasantly surprised to learn how you can be set free from living as a hypocritical Christian and become a vibrant child of God by humbly repenting of your sins and allowing the Kingdom and the will of God to work in you, as it is in Heaven. I wish I had this book during my early years of Christianity.

Jack Mamo, Author of *The Marriage Code Book*; Speaker and Coach

In her book, Leslie opens up her heart, allowing the reader to see how God has brought healing and restoration in a way that only He can do. Regardless of where you have been, Leslie provides a message of hope and healing, having personally experienced that "His grace is sufficient."

Linda Olson, CEO of Wealth Through Stories, www.wealththroughstories.com; Author of Amazon #1 Bestseller, *His Ways Are Higher: One Woman's Journey of Self-Forgiveness Against Unbeatable Odds*

Leslie's book reminds us of the very thing that qualifies each one of us for God's grace: sin and brokenness. With every page of Leslie's story, I am thanking God for the grace that saved me, the grace that is transforming me, one day at a time. It's thrilling to know that we, too, can walk in the joy and freedom that has been made fully available to all of us through the finished work of Jesus.

Neil Boron, Host of LifeLine on WDCX Radio, 99.5 FM, Buffalo, N.Y.

I applaud Leslie's courage as she recounts her tale of "Relational Recklessness". With genuine and complete vulnerability, she shares her journey of waywardness, complete despair, recognition of her wrongdoing, and her ultimate decision to take full responsibility for her life choices. The path to making the necessary changes in her heart and life is a stunning depiction of God's redeeming power, His unconditional love, and His never-ending patience. I thank you and respect you, Leslie, for such honesty!

Margie McIntyre, Author of *Mind Matters – Change Your Mind, Change Your Life!* President of the Board of Directors for Masquerade Ministries – "Freedom From Domestic Abuse Through Hope and Grace"

Without Excuse is a very raw and candid story about Leslie's personal struggle with wanting to fill a void in her life that only Jesus can fill. It's a very honest account of her struggle to find love, acceptance, and fulfillment in everything other than Jesus, and how her failed marriages and relationships led her to where she is today – truly finding a relationship with our Father God. Leslie not only found Jesus, but He transformed her with the realization that **He – Is – Enough**. No matter what you're struggling with, this book and story will help you through. It's filled with Scripture and hope in a world that is so very fallen. Thank you, Leslie, for sharing your personal struggle. I honestly couldn't put this book down.

Robbie Raugh, R.N. Integrative Nutritionist; Radio Host of The Raw Truth on WDCX Radio 99.5 FM, Buffalo, N.Y.; Health and Fitness Expert seen on ABC TV, ESPN, & 100 Huntley Street; Author of *The Raw Truth Recharge – 7 Truths to Health & Fitness*
www.robbieraugh.com

If you are looking for peace and lasting freedom from the bondage of sin, this book if for you. Beautifully crafted and a joy to read, Leslie, through her experiences, will guide you toward the greatest adventure there is – a life lived securely in God's Forgiveness, Will, and Love.

Suzanne D. Jubb, #1 Amazon Bestselling Author of *The Golden Goose, One Important Step to Financial Freedom*

Leslie was willing to take the mask off and, at the same time, allow Christ to do His work in her heart and life. The courage and boldness in this book is God's answer to your healing! Her articulate candor will challenge you to face yourself, your sins, and your demons. If you utilize the tools, reflections, and questions along with the Word of God and a personal relationship with Him, it will stimulate you through a healing journey. Thank you, Leslie, for writing this God-inspired, anointed book. Buy two—one for yourself and one for a friend!

Linda Penn, WDCX (99.5 FM) Radio Host of Today's Living Hope, Saturdays 1-3 PM; Bible Teacher and Biblical Counselor

Leslie Smith, a success in her own right, opens up to reveal the secret shame of who she once was and how relational recklessness held her bound and captive to negative patterns and mindsets. Getting to the root of her dysfunction, Leslie shares openly, honestly, and with deep conviction. This book provides insight, direction, and hope to those struggling with relationship issues and the sin habits that contribute to them. Above all, it leads each reader to the One who has all the answers.

Kate Janzen, Author of *Moving Forward After Betrayal*; www.movingforwardafterbetrayal.com; kate.janzen2015@gmail.com

I have had the pleasure of attending events where Leslie was the main speaker. You leave feeling more informed after listening to her speak. Leslie is very knowledgeable, eloquent yet "real" with words, keeps your interest, and leaves you desiring to hear more from her, including not being able to put her book down until you are finished!

Bev Burton, Author of soon-to-be-released book *Create Your Calm Waters*; Co-author of *Walking in Your Destiny, Living in His Increase* and *Walking in Your Destiny, Abiding in Revival*

Without Excuse

Saying "No!" to Relational Recklessness

Leslie J. Smith

Without Excuse—Saying "No!" to Relational Recklessness

Copyright © 2017 by Leslie J. Smith Professional Corporation

Design and Layout by: ChristianAuthorsGetPaid.com

Editor: Cheryl Regier, Zachariah House @ zachariahhouseofhelps@gmail.com

All rights reserved. No part of this publication may be reproduced or transmitted in any form, in part or in whole, without prior written permission from Leslie J. Smith Professional Corporation, except in the case of a reviewer who may quote limited passages for review purposes only.

Written requests for reproduction must be sent to:

Leslie J. Smith Professional Corporation

1540 Cornwall Road, Suite 105

Oakville, ON L6J 7W5

Tel: 905-467-0280

ljsmith@cogeco.ca

Scripture quotations are from The Holy Bible, English Standard Version® (ESV®), copyright © 2001 by Crossway, a publishing ministry of Good News Publishers. Used by permission. All rights reserved.

Scripture quotations marked NKJV are taken from the New King James Version. Copyright © 1982 by Thomas Nelson, Inc. Used by permission. All rights reserved.

Printed in the United States of America

ISBN: 978-0-9919707-2-8

DEDICATION

This book is dedicated to Jesus Christ,
my Lord and Savior,
who once again rescued me
from the pit that I had dug for myself.

ACKNOWLEDGEMENTS

No one publishes a book by themselves, and that has certainly been true for me.

I first want to express my deepest gratitude to Kathleen D. Mailer, my book shepherd, dear friend, and mentor. Who would have guessed when we met in 2012 that I would now be publishing my second book under your watchful eye? Thank you, Dear Sister in Christ, for your encouragement, friendship, and professional advice throughout this project. Your light shines brightly wherever you go! I praise God for you and Dan and for all that you do for so many!

Secondly, I express my profound gratitude to my editor, Mrs. Cheryl Regier. This was our first time working together but will certainly not be the last! I thought I was a good writer until I read your edits on my first manu-script. Do you ever know what you are doing! Thank you for your perseverance along with your keen eye for detail, formatting, copy-right issues, flow, grammar, and readability. On top of all that, your solid belief, knowledge of Scriptures, and Godly wisdom have been indispensable. My book reads well because of you. Thank you also for encouraging me to finish this book. Mostly, I thank God that I met you and count you as my friend.

Thirdly, I am deeply grateful to the Christian brothers and sisters God brought into my life throughout my walk as a Believer. Thank you to all who have cared about me and for me. Your prayers have kept me going through the toughest of times. There is truly nothing in this world better than Christian fellowship. I am surely blessed!

Finally, but not least, I thank God for my parents, especially my dear father who passed away while I wrote this book. I love you, Dad, with all my heart, and I know that you loved me, too. As I got older, we had some wonderful times together with lots of laughs. You were a wonderful father even with your imperfections. You taught me how to think and to be responsible. You taught me to never quit and to work hard. You did what was right, instead of what was expedient. You loved Jesus in your quiet way. You were unwaveringly faithful, true, dependable, protective, and unafraid to discipline us. You were faithful to Mum and a wonderful provider. I miss you but rejoice in the fact that we will see each other again in the presence of Jesus.

To all of you, *thank you* for all that you have invested in me that made this book possible.

FOREWORD

Ours is a culture of contradiction.

On the one hand, we crave and celebrate authenticity, while on the other, we hide and protect our flaws and vulnerabilities, fearing the consequences of others discovering what we know to be the truth about ourselves.

Having spent nearly thirty years in local church leadership, I have observed that followers of Jesus, for the most part, are not exempt from the fears or risks associated with authenticity. In fact, church culture itself sometimes creates a heightened, spiritual protectionism by emphasizing that Jesus' followers should have it all together. This reality, rather than contributing to personal transparency and congregational health, has instead inspired superficiality and affectation.

Conversely, the church thrives when there is freedom among those who follow Jesus to be honest about their flaws, brokenness, and dysfunction, and embrace truth, repentance, and authenticity. It is only when we come to grips with the truth about our shortcomings and sinfulness that we can receive and experience the life changing grace and mercy of God. It is only when the sin in our lives is exposed can we embrace God's plan and purpose for our lives and know the joy that can be found in Him alone.

In the chapters that follow, Leslie Smith will pull back the curtain of her life and allow us all a glimpse into her spiritual journey, choosing to risk rejection and her reputation as she shares openly about her mistake-ridden past and how God has gracefully and mercifully changed her life.

Without Excuse – Saying "No!" to Relational Recklessness is not a tabloid revelation of the mistakes, brokenness, struggles, and sinfulness of Leslie's life. It is an account of a woman coming to grips with the truth about herself and her sin, her testimony of how God has restored her life, and most importantly, a call for others to experience the same. Leslie's vulnerability will help us objectively analyze why we find ourselves in sin and will lovingly bring us to the place of repentance, revival, and restoration.

Thank you, Leslie, for having the courage to write these pages, giving us an insight into the most personal struggles of your life and for allowing us to celebrate with you the life changing power of God. Your passion to see others overcome their sin by the grace of God and embrace their full potential for Him saturates this work. May this book inspire all who read it to live lives unspoiled by sin and defeat, finding encouragement and hope in Him.

W. Shannon Potter, BTh., MTS

Lead Pastor

Evangel Pentecostal Church

TABLE OF CONTENTS

Introduction 1

Chapter 1: Through the Looking Glass..........11

Chapter 2: Just the Facts, Ma'am...................17

Chapter 3: The Why Behind the Why............35

Chapter 4: A Long Way from Home................45

Chapter 5: The Spirit of Loneliness...............59

Chapter 6: Compassion of Jesus.....................73

Chapter 7: Into the Light................................93

Chapter 8: Enemy at the Gate......................105

Chapter 9: King, Interrupted.......................125

Chapter 10: The Keys to Restoration..........145

Chapter 11: Putting It All Together.............171

Chapter 12: The Big Picture........................191

About the Author..209

INTRODUCTION

*"We all have chapters
that we would rather keep unpublished."*

Robert Crawley, Earl of Grantham
Downtown Abbey

* * * * * * * * *

*"In a futile attempt to erase our past,
we deprive the community of our healing gift.
If we conceal our wounds out of fear and shame,
our inner darkness can neither be illuminated
nor become a light for others."*

Brennan Manning,
*Abba's Child: The Cry of the Heart for Intimate
Belonging*

Lord Grantham would likely have told me not to publish this book. Brennan Manning would have said the opposite.

My carnal and prideful self does not want to tell this story. It happens to be a very long chapter in my life, one of which I am not proud. To publish this book, so I have said to myself, is to put at risk my reputation, one that I have carefully crafted since becoming a believer in 2001.

Can you hear the pride in my words?

Satan does not want this book published because in it, I expose him and his schemes that have played a leading role in my life for far too long. No, Satan wants me to walk in defeat and render me useless for the work that God has for me to do. He wants to silence anyone – me included – who would speak up for truth and freedom.

Jesus, on the other hand, is all about truth and freedom. He desires that this book be published because it will show you *who He is* in all His Glory and Grace and how His perfect love and healing can be yours for the asking, as it was mine.

Such was my choice. I could hide my story and save my reputation, and thus cooperate with the plans of the enemy, OR I could risk my reputation for the sake of showing off Jesus for the Redeemer that He is and bring healing and freedom to others.

I obviously chose the latter. Whatever I may or may not endure, I will know that Jesus is given His rightful place as Lord and Savior in my life, and I pray, in yours as well. This is really His story through me.

There is a lot at stake when we sin. It's not just that we wreak havoc in our own lives and damage our witness. When we sin, we take our eyes and our worship off God. And in that momentary falter, we open ourselves up to the wiles of the enemy whose primary task in our lives is to distract us from our mission to further God's Kingdom. Through sin, we hand over to Satan the territory and influence that God has given us, we mar our walk with Christ, and we frustrate our God-given destiny and the purposes for which God created us. Satan knows that we can't serve the Kingdom when we are turned inward and focusing on ourselves or on that thing we are pursuing that we have turned into an idol.

From personal experience, I know that when a believer sins, Satan puts fear into our minds and hearts, convincing us that if we ask for help from our church or fellow believers, we will be judged, ostracized, gossiped about, or run out of the church. In addition, we fear we will lose our reputation in the community or in our business. Consequently, it is understandable that many believers who deserve healing and restoration shy away from seeking the help that is available.

This does not have to happen to you.

Through the telling of my story in this book, I believe that God is attempting to accomplish two things.

Firstly, God is reaching out to believers who may be suffering the effects of sin in their life. He wants us to stop and assess our circumstances and confront ourselves. How did we get into this present situation?

This book will help us objectively analyze why we find ourselves in sin and will lovingly bring us to the place of repentance, revival, and restoration. Our God wants us to know that there is Grace and Mercy available for us if we would only repent and turn from our sin. Therein lies the freedom and peace in our hearts that we are all desperately seeking.

Secondly, God wants those reading this book that may not be walking in sin at the moment to be filled with God's compassion for those who are suffering in their sin. God wants to do a work in our hearts in the area of extending Mercy and Grace to our fellow believers while leaving the judgment part to Him. And yes, understanding that "to sin is to suffer" is part of being compassionate.

I pray that my story of walking in sin as a believer will deepen your understanding of how we get ourselves into these situations in the first place. Yet, through the power of the Holy Spirit and the prayers of the saints, we can escape the terrible weight and distraction of sin and step back into a victorious and focused walk with God. This is the hope and the passion that is behind the writing of this book.

Now, you may be saying, *"But you don't know what I've done! I can't face myself, and I surely don't want others to find out about my shame!"*

Let me give you a gentle reminder. God knows *everything* that we've done or are contemplating doing. He knows our every thought before we think it and our every word before we speak it. He sees all the good, the bad, and embarrassing things we do and think. Yet, despite our deepest and darkest of failures and offences, He loves us unconditionally and has Grace and Mercy ready and available for us when we humbly repent and seek His refining fire. Furthermore, He intends to use our struggles for His Glory in the furtherance of His Kingdom.

When we repent and turn from our sinful ways, Jesus runs out to meet us on the pathway home like the father sprinting out to meet his prodigal son.[1] Oh, what a Savior! Even I do not completely understand this

---
[1] Luke 15:11-32

kind of Love...but I know it is real. I have experienced it from the depths of the pit I dug for myself. This Love is crazy and mysterious as well as lovely and awesome all at the same time.

My heart's greatest desire for you is that, through my story, you will see yourself as Jesus sees you: a beloved and chosen child who stumbled and fell. I pray that you will stop running from God's Truth and your humanity. Instead, allow Jesus to restore you and take away the shame, guilt, and self-loathing that you have been burdened with, just as He did for me.

I also pray that my transparency will encourage you to admit to yourself when and where you have strayed from the straight and narrow way. It is time to acknowledge your hourly dependence upon the Lord for His Justice, Grace, and Mercy. I pray that you come to know that acknowledging your need of God's Grace and Mercy is not a sign of weakness but one of great strength and wisdom.

Restoration in Christ is free for the one who genuinely asks. My prayer is that you would so ask. May you hunger and thirst after Him as though your life depended on it because, in fact, it does.

So, let's begin by answering a few questions...

Do you want to be free of the soul-crushing burden of sin and shame? Do you want to be set free from the degradation that you keep putting yourself through? Do you want to walk in newness of life in Christ with a clean heart, a clear mind, and on target with your worship and adoration of God? Do you want to finish this race well? *If you do, then we will do this together!*

This is what I believe Jesus would say to you at this moment:

> *"My Beloved, I see you and know everything about you. Even so, I love you with an unending, furious Love that you will never fully comprehend. I have waited patiently for you. You are My Beloved. I planned you and your purpose before you were born,*

and I will walk with you no matter where you go or what you do. I will help you stay on the straight and narrow path if you let Me. I will, as many times as necessary, stand you up and set your feet firmly upon Me, the Rock of your Salvation. I Am your Grace, Mercy, and Justice. I Am your Shepherd, your Fortress, and your Lighthouse in the dark. I Am your Protector and Provider.

"If you sincerely turn from your sinful ways, you shall have My Peace that no man or woman can fathom. Then, you shall fulfill the plans and purposes for which I specifically handcrafted you. You are the only person in the world who can fulfill those plans and purposes I have designed for you.

"You are safe with Me. So, let's disconnect from the world for a time and figure this thing out once and for all. Then, we will reconnect more intimately than before and begin anew on the path of righteousness for My Name's sake."

It's time to live life without excuse, leaning firmly on the One who can help you in all things, even the elimination of deep-rooted sin habits. Join me in the following chapters as I show you how. Together, we will explore how and why we stepped into sin and gave in to our flesh or selfish desires. We will examine afresh the events that took place in the Garden of Eden and in King David's palace. Most importantly, we will discuss concrete steps to employ in order to avoid giving in to our flesh so that we can finish the race well, as the Apostle Paul encourages us to do!

Leslie

1

THROUGH THE LOOKING GLASS

Despite having been saved by my Redeemer in 2001, I have sinned in many ways and at many times since then. No one is immediately transformed once saved. It is a process. However, I struggled with a number of sins that wanted to keep me addicted to my old nature...one that was *not* part of who I was in Jesus.

My list of transgressions was endless and tiresome. I have harboured anger in my heart towards individuals or muttered obscenities when I have been frustrated. I have been impatient with a loved one or a client, displaying a quick temper and a sharp, acid tongue that has gotten the better of me at the office. I have turned my back on people who have needed help. Selfish pride has kept me distant from people or caused me to refuse to look within at my own shortcomings. I have considered myself better than others because of my education. Bitterness has taken root, I have felt sorry for myself, I have been judgmental, I have over-spent, I have succumbed to covetousness, and more. Despite being saved, I was still indulging in sinful behaviours and habits that were holding me captive.

Most of the time, I would do these things without stopping and analyzing why I was reacting the way I was. Always and without fail, I felt badly afterwards. Furthermore, I once believed that certain types of sins – sins of the heart that no one could see – were not all that serious. Of course, this was wrong thinking on my part.

When I engaged in sin, I failed to go to God first. In addition, I neglected to seek help from brothers and sisters of the faith for fear of judgment, although I may well have received quite the opposite. Such was the subliminal urging of Satan who invaded my mind with the thought that, "*No one will understand.*" This, my friend, is how the enemy slinks in, divides, and conquers…and how we seriously hinder our walk with God.

In some cases, I didn't seek help because I did not want to stop walking in sin. This was primarily because I was getting something out of it. Specifically, the sin was feeding my sense of selfishness or some deficit in my soul or psyche that I did not understand. And of course, most sin is downright pleasurable, so stopping it involves pain and disappointment, feelings that are abhorrent to most of us.

I was saved in 2001 at the age of 44 years. Shortly after I was saved, I had a very brief affair with a married man. A number of years later, I did the same thing again with another married man. The second relationship lasted longer and was extremely painful to disconnect from.

The Word tells us that the flesh wants what the flesh wants.[2] I can personally attest that this is most certainly true. For some people, temptation in this area of sexual sin feels like it is impossible to resist.

Sexual sin is as old as time itself, and the Bible is very clear that it is a sin. Yet, despite Scriptures of warning and direction on how to live uprightly, good people with otherwise unblemished lives can find themselves involved in it and, in some cases, addicted to it.

I liken sexual sin to a crop of dandelions on your front lawn; you can't eradicate the crop by simply cutting the tops off the dandelions with the lawnmower. Instead, you need to employ preventive measures like spraying the lawn with dandelion-killer, laying down grass seed, and digging the plant out by its

---

[2] See Galatians 5:17

roots the moment it rears its ugly head above the surface of the earth. It's a continual and never-ending process that you must stay on top of.

I suspect that many believers are desperate for help and direction from their church and fellow believers on real issues like sexual sin. When we are struggling with something that has us in a vice-grip, we need help. Similarly, as in the case of a person diagnosed with cancer, aggressive help is often required.

All sin, including sexual sin, is a cancer of the spirit. Those suffering with whatever sin they are walking in require spiritual chemotherapy. This involves taking a hard look in the mirror, having a reality check, genuine repentance, honest accountability, the prayer support of the saints, and the Lord's supernatural deliverance. Sometimes, we need the spiritual equivalent of shock treatment where we receive a serious jolt of conviction that brings us back to the reality of what we are doing, how detrimental it is to our spiritual health and overall wellbeing, and how far off the path we have wandered.

It is imperative that we engage in a pre-emptive strike against Satan through prayer and fasting and digesting the Word. We need a skillful Surgeon with a very sharp blade because the problem, when advanced to full realization, is deep and complicated and can reappear like dandelions on the front lawn.

As a first step toward saying "no" to sin, we must understand and discern how and why we decided to point our feet toward that path of self-destruction in the first place. This involves an investigation into the facts.

2

JUST THE FACTS, MA'AM

When I stopped and analyzed the facts, I realized that over the course of most of my life, I have struggled with what author Melody Beattie would describe as "codependency". Codependency is described as "a psychological condition or a relationship in which a person manifesting a low self-esteem or a strong desire for approval has an unhealthy attachment to another person and places the needs of that person before his or her own. In co-dependency, a person tries to satisfy the needs of another who is often controlling or manipulative and who may have an addictive or emotionally unstable personality."[3]

---

[3] www.merriam-webster.com

Therefore, codependency is expressed through unsuccessful and unhealthy relationships where one or both parties have unresolved emotional and self-esteem issues.

My personal life paints a rather unflattering picture. I had many boyfriends in high school, have suffered through two failed marriages, had a couple of very brief, extramarital flings while I was married, and indulged in relationships with married men as a single woman that included two after I was saved. My personal life has personified dysfunction, selfishness, and recklessness.

Whatever it was inside of me that led me to this behaviour before I was saved continued to fester below the surface after my salvation. Despite my genuine profession of faith, I hadn't yet discovered what was causing such havoc in my personal relationships. The root system had not yet been cut out.

Meeting Jesus in 2001

I remember the moment like it was yesterday.

A few days after my latest relationship failed, I was on the computer. Suddenly, the word "crucifixion" came to my mind. I had gone to church as a child but fell away in high school, so why this word was dropped into my mind was, at the time, a mystery. I had never been all that interested in Jesus up until that point.

I performed a search on the word, clicking on an article that appeared to be a medical description of the suffering and crucifixion of Jesus. I understood every medical term and gruesome description in that article. As it happened, the highest mark I ever received in any class that I took was in my university physiology class (98%), a fact that apparently had not escaped the notice of Jesus.

As I read what this doctor was describing, I envisioned the entire scene in my active imagination. I didn't need to see a movie of it.

I "saw" the horror of it through that doctor's description, and I wept at the cruelty that Jesus had to suffer through.

My heart broke! Jesus, who I somehow knew in my heart was a gentle man, had been treated with utter contempt, disregard, and hatred. As recorded in Isaiah 52:14, Jesus' body was reduced to an appalling disfigured form, marred beyond human likeness. He was abused, tortured, and killed without due process.[4] Certainly, the medical description in this doctor's article appeared to accurately support descriptions in the Word of God.

As a mother, I could not help but weep thinking about how Mary must have felt as she watched her son's suffering. As a lawyer, anger boiled up inside of me with knowledge that Jesus was denied an automatic appeal for a crime that called for the death penalty simply because he was not a Roman citizen. As a student of physiology, I realized it was a medical miracle that He lasted long enough to have been raised up on that old, rugged

---

[4] See Isaiah 53:3-9

cross. For the most part, as a sinner – with eyes opened to the reality of the Lord's sacrifice – my heart broke wide open.

Compelled by an unseen force, I finished reading the article, after which I went into my bedroom's walk-in closet, sank to the floor on my knees, and wept for my lifetime of sin. A bad movie of my life played in my mind while Jesus showed me how I had hurt others and myself through my relational recklessness and sexual sin. I felt the weight of conviction and sorrow over how I had wounded Jesus on the cross. Oddly enough, I did not experience the familiar, sharp jabs of guilt over my secret shame. Instead, I felt Jesus comforting me while showing me my own iniquities.

Who was this Jesus?

In that dark closet, I begged God to forgive me of my sins and to take over my life and run it. Why I did that was a mystery to me. No one had previously told me what to do or say. I just did it.

After about an hour or so, I stood up feeling a thousand pounds lighter. My tears had dried, and my heart experienced a peace that I had never before known. As I would come to understand later, the Holy Spirit had washed over me and downloaded Grace and Mercy into every part of my being. I experienced that confounding, perfect love of Jesus that healed and saved. He set me up on my feet to walk in newness of life.

The morning after I committed my life to Christ, I remember waking up feeling fully and completely loved in a way I had never before experienced with a boy or a man or even my parents. That pervasive, damp fog of loneliness and unworthiness that had covered me like my own skin had lifted. I thanked Jesus for making me clean and whole.

I pledged to be done with my old life of playing the impetuous, reckless fool. More than anything, I wanted to be whole in my body. I sought to take it back and treat it for what it was – a gift from God to be kept pure for His purpose and as a temple where the Holy Spirit resides. It was my desire to keep

His temple clean and undefiled out of absolute reverence for Jesus and what He had endured on the cross for me.

As a result, when I stumbled and fell back into old habits later on, I was completely disheartened. I imagine this may be what recovering alcoholics must feel like when, after years of sobriety, they succumb to the temptation and take a drink once again, leaving their progress and good intentions in ruins at their feet. I was deeply disappointed in myself, feeling incredibly low and hopeless.

Would I ever beat this problem? Would I ever stop acting like the Samaritan woman at the well?[5]

What I did not fully realize at the time was that the walk of a believer is the walk of crucifying the flesh, that is, our own selfish way of doing things. When we commit our lives to Jesus through our confession of faith, our spirit is saved. However, our flesh still needs to undergo a transformation, and we

---
[5] See John 4:1-26

are called to daily die to self, as hard as that is. With Jesus as Lord in our life, this dying to self is now possible. It is a journey of walking out our faith and being transformed through God's Grace.

Despite my genuine and sincere confession of faith and my otherwise faithful walk with God, the hidden root system of my habitual, life-long, relational recklessness was still in place below the surface. Like the dandelions I mentioned earlier, I had deep-rooted habits in my life that needed to come out. My character possessed a defect that Satan knew well how to exploit. As a new Christian, I had yet to see this area of weakness transformed and renewed.

The Apostle Paul explained it best when he wrote:

For we know that the law is spiritual, but I am of the flesh, sold under sin. For I do not understand my own actions. For I do not do what I want, but I do the very thing I hate. Now if I do what I do not want, I agree with the law, that it is good. So now it is no longer I who do it, but sin that dwells within me. For I know that nothing good dwells in me, that is, in my flesh. For I have the desire to do what is right, but not the ability to carry it out. For I do not do the good I want, but the evil I do not want is what I keep on doing. Now if I do what I do not want, it is no longer I who do it, but sin that dwells within me.

So I find it to be a law that when I want to do right, evil lies close at hand. For I delight in the law of God, in my inner being, but I see in my members another law waging war against the law of my mind and making me captive to the law of sin that dwells in my members. Wretched man that I am! Who will deliver me from this body of death? Thanks be to God through Jesus Christ our Lord! So then, I myself serve the law of God with my mind, but with my flesh I serve the law of sin.

~ Romans 7:14-25

Satan presented me with an invitation in the form of a married man, and I allowed sin to entice me and take control. I entertained the temptation and ignored that little voice inside of me that said, *"Don't!"* Justifying the sin in my mind, I birthed the idea into action.

I opened the door just a crack...and in rolled the fog, filling and polluting my entire house. I abandoned the biblical teaching that had been placed in my heart, choosing instead to indulge my flesh and do things my way. I listened to the low, vile whispers of the enemy telling me that, "*No one will ever know.*"

Pivotal to my decision to take up with a married man was my internal rationalization of it. It went something like this:

No relationship in my life has lasted, including two marriages. I am lonely. I have devoted myself to God after being saved in 2001, and yet I am still single. Didn't He say in Genesis that man should not be alone? So why am I still alone? Wasn't God supposed to bring me my promised mate? Quite obviously, God doesn't really care about me because, if He did, He would have brought me a mate by now.
So, if God doesn't care about me, then I won't care about Him. I won't read Your Word, God. I won't seek advice or help from leaders in my church because they will just make me stop seeing this married man...and I don't want to

stop. I won't go to church, or if I go, I won't listen. I will take matters into my own hands and indulge myself because this is what I need and deserve. I can handle this from here, God. Thanks anyway. I'll call you if I need You.

Can you see how my thinking was all about me and how utterly self-centred my heart was? I had abandoned the God who had rescued me from my hell on earth and worse. Furthermore, I had accused Him of wrongdoing.

Like Eve whose perspective was totally self-centred, I deceived myself and made a conscious decision to disobey God, take of the forbidden "fruit"[6], and have it my way. I then blamed God for my own destruction knowing all the while that, as a believer, I was the offender having rejected God's laws.

I bought the enemy's lies – hook, line, and sinker. I justified the thing that I had convinced myself I needed and deserved. I attempted to replace the perfect love,

---

[6] Genesis 3:1-7

comfort, and protective covering of Jesus and the Holy Spirit with a cheap, counterfeit imitation.

I had strayed a long, long way from my new home in Jesus.

Those who know my walk with the Lord might be surprised to read these things. Yet, it shouldn't come as a surprise. We are all masters at hiding the ugly parts of ourselves, showing only what we want others to see, especially at church and in the presence of our fellow believers.

I thank God for eventually showing me how and why my personal life had become such a series of unfortunate events by my own hand. We will get into more of my story in the next chapter. First, let's begin at the beginning. If we are ever going to break the strongholds and chains that bind us and take us out of living a victorious life according to God's will, we have to first acknowledge how we steered our lives into the ditch and why.

The first step, therefore, is to stop and objectively assess the situation. For myself, I needed to wake up out of my stupor and stop and take a hard and honest look at my life. No longer could I excuse my conduct. I had to face the facts.

Secondly, it was essential for me to establish the baseline. This meant I needed to record exactly what I was doing, no matter how hard that exercise was. If we do not know where we currently are and why we are stuck there (the baseline), we cannot chart a path to where we want to go.

If you are sick and tired of walking a defeated life in persistent sin, then take a moment to pray and ask Jesus to show you where you are going astray and why. Ask Him to lead you into His Truth. Today is the day to put a stake in the ground and say "NO!" to relational recklessness or whatever other plaguing sin has you in its grip.

If you want to make a permanent change in the way you are doing business with God, if you want to stop living in defeat, if you want to experience lasting freedom from the bondage of sin, then decide right now to put an end to it. Open your heart to receive the gifts of Grace, Mercy, and Healing in your life, which will, in turn, lead you to a God-blessed life instead of a life filled with defeat and degradation and failure. Jesus did not willingly endure the horrors of Good Friday for any of us to slog along in defeat and ruination by our own hand.

Let's Pray:

Thank you, God, that You are Sovereign and that you see all and know all. Thank you that You love me above and beyond all understanding and above and beyond my sinful ways. Please open the eyes of my heart to myself. Show me what I need to see about myself right now, and give me Your strength to be honest about my life and the sin I am walking in. I declare that I can do this work through the guidance and healing power of Christ Jesus, my Lord and Savior. In Jesus' Name. Amen.

Reflection – Stop and Assess the Situation

1.　List each and every situation that is described in the Bible as sin that you are currently in, were involved in, or are contemplating. Include in this list the sins against God (idolatry, taking the Lord's name in vain, worshipping other gods, not honouring the Sabbath), sins of the heart (anger, lust, lying, hatred, disharmony, foul speech, envy, covetousness, being judgmental, etc.), any sexual sins (fornication, adultery, pornography, sexual abuse), or other sins such as theft, forgery, fraud, assault, etc. If you need reminding, read the Ten Commandments in Exodus 20 and Galatians 5:19-21. There are other passages in the Bible that describe sin as well. Make a list of everything you were or are now involved in. Do not judge yourself or your answers because it may prevent you from being honest. Just objectively record the facts in the same way that you make a grocery list.

2.　Beside each instance of sin, describe how you think you will benefit from what you are doing? Don't worry about how intellectually challenged your answers might sound or how foolish you might feel. Again, do not judge yourself. Remember that, right now, you are simply recording the facts.

3. Spend some time meditating on the Scripture below and notice how Jesus dealt with the woman caught in adultery. Observe His straightforward and clear directive to her to go and stop sinning. Notice the lack of shaming and ridicule. He gave no long explanations or lectures, no finger wagging, nagging, or harassment. Jesus simply said, *"go and...sin no more."*

This they said to test him, that they might have some charge to bring against him. Jesus bent down and wrote with his finger on the ground. And as they continued to ask him, he stood up and said to them, "Let him who is without sin among you be the first to throw a stone at her." And once more he bent down and wrote on the ground. But when they heard it, they went away one by one, beginning with the older ones, and Jesus was left alone with the woman standing before him. Jesus stood up and said to her, "Woman, where are they? Has no one condemned you?"

She said, "No one, Lord." And Jesus said, "Neither do I condemn you; go, and from now on sin no more."
~ John 8:6-11

4. Reflect also on Jesus's admonition directed to church leaders who were filled with judgment and hatred for the woman in the above passage. Judgment and hatred do not lead people to repentance. It is the job of the Body of Christ to let the Word and the Holy Spirit convict, and instead of judgment, show compassion to those struggling with sin that they may be supported in the choice to repent.

3

THE WHY BEHIND THE WHY

As I have confessed, I have engaged in relational and sexual sin as a believer. My "why" or justification for my past actions was my life-long relationship failures and persistent loneliness. If I had stopped the inquiry at this point, telling myself that I needed to simply quit these negative thoughts and behaviors and lean more into Jesus instead (as good and proper as that sounds), there would have been a good chance that I would have continued to engage in this kind of conduct. Why? Without a thorough and honest introspection, I would not have dug down to the roots of these issues and removed them from my life.

I could've prayed and asked God to remove these things from my life. But what are "these things"? What, besides my selfish pursuits of things of the flesh and my obvious failure to fix my gaze upon Jesus and abide in Him, was the root cause of the habits that tempted me? What was buried deep inside my heart and soul that had caused me to engage in self-destructive ways for most of my life? What did I need to discover about myself that I had previously ignored or been blind to?

Surely, these were valid questions that deserved to be answered. Had I dismissed these questions and refused to do the work that would reveal my inner workings, I would have been in danger of merely cutting the top off the dandelions – the problem – rather than excavating them out by the root. Therefore, it was necessary for me to go deeper still and ask myself a few pivotal questions. They included soul-searching and hard questions like the following:

1.   Why have I been unable to establish a successful relationship?

2.   Why have I given in to sexual sin as a believer when I know perfectly well it is an offence in God's eyes?

3. What knee-jerk or deeply ingrained habits, thought patterns, or emotional or psychological deficits, have gripped me so tightly that I so readily give myself license to choose wrongly? *It was critical for me to uncover my "why behind the why?"*

As you read my account, you may wish to reflect upon your own "family of origin" issues.

Beginnings

I came from a good home where my sibling and I were safe and secure and loved. Life was peaceful if not boring. My parents were fine, upstanding, and successful people.

My father, a professional engineer, was a prosperous businessman. Through his hard work and dedication, he earned a very comfortable living for his family. He was a faithful husband, father, protector, provider, and disciplinarian to a fault.

Mother was a homemaker of excellence. She had a soft heart, especially when we kids were upset about something. Outside of the home, she volunteered at the hospital and at church. However, she always made sure that things at home were her first priority.

Indeed, we came from an excellent home by most people's standards. From the outside looking in, we lacked nothing. Everything was in order. However, even the best of families have their areas of dysfunction.

My father was an intelligent, quiet, reserved, and introverted man who never uttered a word without carefully considering it. Not once did I ever hear him say anything off the cuff or ill conceived. He held a multitude of opinions and judgments about things and about people. On those topics, we knew where he stood beyond a shadow of a doubt. Of his personal feelings, especially towards his family, we heard nothing.

Dad seemed to have a somewhat pessimistic outlook towards me. I suspect he would have described his viewpoint as being "realistic" as opposed to negative. By never being optimistic, he shielded himself and his family from disappointment.

My dad also preferred things to be orderly and predictable. I suppose this made him feel safe, and especially so if he could orchestrate things in such a way as to accomplish what he most likely felt was a secure world. Furthermore, he saw this as part of his role as protector and provider.

My mother once told me that Dad didn't know how to deal with a girl…so he kept his emotional distance from me. I certainly never felt like "Daddy's little girl", a coveted position that many of my friends enjoyed. I never found my "home" in my father's heart, although I desperately wanted to.

Mostly, I was afraid of my father. Although he was never physically abusive in any way, he was quiet and stern, which I took as a sign that he was disappointed in me. I felt that he disapproved of my sense of frivolity, lightness, and optimism, although I never confirmed that with him. Regardless of what was real or imagined, the silent messages I received and perceived as a child led me to believe that my father was to be feared and that I was a disappointment.

Growing up, we lacked for nothing in the way of material possessions, trips, education, experiences, appropriate discipline, nice clothes, guidance, direction, and more. Of this care, I can find no fault. However, there were very little, if any, verbal expressions of encouragement or joy, especially from my father. Life had a very matter-of-fact quality to it. In our house, the product of our hard work was exalted along with good grades and being polite to the neighbors. All these things related to our outward expressions and presentation. We were absolutely not to do anything whatsoever that would cause the neighbors to gossip about us. Performance for the sake of presenting the "perfect" picture was our life.

As puberty gripped me like darkness heralds the night, the distance between my father and me grew. Eventually, this distance affected my relationship with my mother as well. With my emotions fluctuating up and down by the minute, I couldn't stop feeling sad and angry towards my parents. Truth be told, I made my parents' lives a misery most of the time. There were fights and tears followed by awkward silences that would last for several days at times. I couldn't express myself to them, and in reality, I felt at the time that they would not have known what to do with my feelings even if I had shared them. The disconnect just got worse.

I often felt isolated in my own home. Believing (rightly or wrongly) that my parents were talking about me behind my back, I became overly sensitive and sullen, spending most of my time in my bedroom. I was forever hearing, "*Stop sulking and put a smile on your face!*" I grew to believe that there was something seriously wrong with me because I was experiencing all these emotions in a home where they were not encouraged or accepted.

Expressing one's emotions was an extravagance that likely didn't fit into my parents' upbringings and were not really welcomed in our house. So, I stored all my feelings inside of me where they could at least exist without being rejected or criticized. The hazard of bottling up such powerful emotions, however, was beyond my understanding at the time.

Restlessness began welling up in my heart, and I often found myself wanting to run away. My heart yearned to find some place where I could be around people who would encourage and acknowledge me, not just for how polite I was or how good my grades were, but also for me as a person. My heart's desire was to find a place where I could just "be me" without having to conform to someone else's standards and fear-based thinking. I craved an environment where people had joy in their hearts and were not afraid to express it and could thus accept that I, too, had emotions that needed to come out in order for me to be happy. Subsequently, I found my "home" at school and in other people's houses, and I actually felt closer to some of my friends' parents than to my own.

There was another reason why I sincerely believed there was something wrong with me. My father never, not once, told me I was beautiful or smart or lovely just as I was. I always wondered why he could not sweep me up in his arms and tell me that he loved me more than any other girl in the whole wide world. The affirmation and affection that a girl needs from her father was missing in my life.

Feeling completely rejected, I could not tell my dad what I needed from him. Instead, I stepped out in defiance into a path of rebellion doing what I knew was against the rules. In my pain, I sought my father's love in all the wrong places and in all the wrong ways.

Please note that my parents did none of this deliberately to hurt me. They knew only what they grew up with, especially in a generation where outward displays of emotion and affection were frowned upon. They operated from their own places of strengths and sufficiency, as well as weaknesses and deficiencies, much of it learned behavior based on upbringing and an absence of understanding. Faultfinding is, therefore, not the point of this part of my story. The point is to understand the contributing factors to how my emotional make-up was developed.

The rest of my story is a description of the choices that I willingly and freely made. They were choices that I knew were contrary to what I had been taught at home. Unfortunately, they led me a long way from home and caused great heartache.

4

A LONG WAY FROM HOME

It was the summer between grade eight and grade nine. I was 14 years old with a huge chip on my shoulder. I was acquainted with several, young men, one of whom was 21 years old. He seemed interested in me for some reason, and naturally, I was flattered. I wasn't used to having a boy interested in me... and it felt really nice. I knew nothing about the dangers that lurked for a young girl inexperienced in the ways of men.

This boy invited me over. He lived in a run-down part of town that was a long way from what I was used to. Red flags went up within my conscience all along that long, hot, bike ride there...but I ignored them. Some sort of expectation kept me cycling towards my fate.

I knocked on the broken, front door that creaked as I opened it. I stepped inside to find him lounging on a ratty, old couch wearing only a housecoat. I knew right then and there that I should leave, but instead, I froze for fear of this boy's rejection and ridicule. I cared more about what he thought about me than I cared about my personal wellbeing. I said and did nothing.

Later, as that young man put another notch in his belt, confusion, shame, and terror echoed in my head as I told myself, "*Tell no one.*" I could not risk my parents' condemnation and anger and rejection, especially remembering my father's singular attempt at sex education: "*If you ever get pregnant, the door will be locked behind you!*"

The event of that infamous day unwittingly impressed upon my heart a sense of emptiness and lack of self-worth that would follow me for decades. From that day onward, I perfected the art of getting the attention and affection of boys by giving them more than I could afford while not guarding my own heart, body, and emotional wellbeing. Such is the mentality of a codependent that has no concept about boundaries.

I proceeded to chase boys in high school, having short relationships of usually no more than three months in length. I would morph into whatever the boy wanted, being too afraid to lose him if I spoke my mind or expressed myself. My main objective was to have a boyfriend who would not reject me. My methods, however, were extremely faulty. I was controlling and manipulative in an effort to ward off any and all rejection.

By the time I left high school, I had developed into a type-A personality awash with low self-esteem, shame, and a complete lack of compassion for others or myself. I was also a perfectionist, a human "doing" instead of a human "being". I silently ridiculed people who were weak-willed, and at the same time, I lacked the self-awareness into my own emotions that led me to be indecisive and easily swayed. For example, I held no opinions on any topic, believing it was better to just agree with whatever anyone said to me. Emotions embarrassed me. My over-developed ego covered up what I inwardly believed about myself: I was a dysfunctional misfit. I became an imposter wearing a mask through all my "doings" to hide the emptiness and loneliness inside of me.

With this elixir of hidden, emotional poison coursing through my veins, I met my first husband at university, and we married when I was just 21 years old. I recall thinking that this would be my way out from being under the control and influence of my parents. I entered that marriage having no understanding of what it meant to make a lifelong commitment.

My first husband was a decent, innocent man with the best of intentions who unwittingly married a hollow, empty, and hurting young woman. Four years later, I detonated that relationship when I met a man at law school who seemed a whole lot more interesting. Marriage counselling did not really help, but I did it for appearances' sake.

Feeling the need to escape my first marriage, I hatched a plan. I would leave him without any explanation and move my belongings out of the house one day while he was at work. Perhaps, I thought, he wouldn't notice. My thoughts were only for myself.

I behaved recklessly, selfishly, and without an ounce of moral integrity or courage. My husband was rocked to his very core. I deeply hurt him, his family, and mine.

At a restaurant no less, I casually informed my mother that I had left him. She was shattered, but her resolve to never make a scene in public assured me that I would not "catch heck". As usual, it was all about me.

I shudder now when I think about the way in which I treated my first husband. I cringe at how I lurched from man to man afterwards, not thinking things through or giving full consideration to the lives that I negatively impacted and harmed. My behavior was completely reprehensible.

I was wilfully reckless with my own life and the lives of those around me.

My father was so mad at me for leaving my first husband that he took the keys to his house away from me, an act that horrified my mother. She feared she would never see me again. However, she said nothing, not wanting to challenge him in front of me. A united front was the order of the day.

My second marriage was self-destructive as well. I was not whole or emotionally healthy, and neither was he. We both had personal issues that we had not dealt with, and it was a poor combination from the outset. To make matters worse, I felt compelled to prove to my parents that I had made the right decision in leaving my first husband...so I stayed.

Trying to force something that should never have happened in the first place, I paid no attention to my own emotional needs until I was so numb inside that I felt nothing. I kept plodding along in my second marriage, primarily for the sake of our children. The emotional dysfunction within the relationship was sucking the life out me.

A friend of mine, who was visiting one night, watched us interact. Afterwards, she asked me if I had any idea how unhappy I was. I was confused by her remarks. Crazy as it sounds, I assumed everybody's marriage was like what I was living through.

My ego drove me to attempt to make the unworkable work, and I stayed longer than I should have. Yet again, my unhealthy need to be loved and not rejected led me to ignore that little voice of warning inside of me. This same voice had told me to stay away from him even before I married him.

I allowed my boundaries to be crossed, and I remained captive behind my own enemy lines.

Inevitably, my second marriage broke up and ended in a bitter divorce. I was left with three children under the age of 7 years, financial difficulties, and emotional ruin. I was 38 years of age.

In therapy, I tried to comprehend how I had gotten to this point in my life, stuck in a place where I did not recognize who I was or where my boundaries were. I needed to understand why I had spent my adult life craving intimacy while having no idea how to achieve it. I knew not why I had spent my life careening from ditch to ditch in my relationships.

Facing the reality of my current situation was a sobering exercise. I vaguely realized that my actions had caused collateral damage along the way, and both my ex-husband and I had negatively affected the lives of three small children, not to mention hurting our extended families. I was faced with the grim picture of what my faulty mentality and poor choices had led to.

Living in a fog where one doesn't know who they are or what they stand for, yet they crave love but push it away at the same time, is one of the symptoms of codependency according to expert and author Melodie Beattie. I desperately needed to come to grips with what I believed and stood for. At that time, I was at a loss as to how to do that.

I cried for about a year after my second marriage imploded until, one night, I got tired of blaming my ex-husband for all my troubles. Instead, I chose to forgive both him and myself for the mess we had caused. Although this was a positive step by itself, my hurt and unhealed soul made a decision moving forward that, in my warped sensibility, seemed to make sense. Believing that I was incapable of making proper decisions with regard to choosing a suitable, life-long mate, I made a pact with myself to never allow any man to get close to me again.

Consequently, I punished myself with a self-imposed exile from the dating scene. Instead, I went in the opposite direction, seeking revenge for what I assumed life had dealt me. I had brief affairs with men I cared little about, believing in some twisted fashion that this way of escape was the answer. I gravitated to married, and thus unavailable men, primarily because they were "safe". They would never be available to have a permanent relationship with me, so I would never have to put myself at risk for more rejection and disappointment. Yet, those casual affairs brought me nothing but pain, shame, and more loneliness.

I craved emotional intimacy but attracted the complete opposite.

Bitterness set in as I unwittingly created the circumstances that brought familiar (albeit unwelcome) emotional responses. I hadn't yet faced my deeper issues or examined that which had created the foundation for my current state. I needed to "come back home" to discover the roots to the negative patterns in my life.

If we are ever to create a healthy reality for ourselves, we need to know who we are, where we have come from, as well as understand what influenced and shaped us initially. We have to take our hands off our eyes and our fingers out of our ears and carefully look and listen within.

Reflection – Stop and Assess the Situation

Take a moment now and think about your own "family of origin" issues and your own emotional make-up. Respond honestly to the questions below. This will greatly assist your understanding of who you are and what areas in your life may be tempting and/or causing you to sin.

1. Write a general, biographical sketch of yourself starting with your birth. Write about what happened to you as a child through to the present time. Record whatever flows out without judgment or editing. No one else will read this. Cover all areas of your life including your family life, school life, relationships, etc. Describe what it was like growing up in your family and your emotions. Describe any expectations you had about yourself or your family members. Describe any "secrets" that you would not want someone else to find out about. What causes you shame and guilt? What happened to you that you wished had not happened? What did you do to someone else that you wish you had not done? This sketch will help to pinpoint areas that may be tied to your current struggle with sin and, in particular, recklessness within your relationships.

2. Write a specific, biographical sketch of yourself focusing on a particular area of your life such as relationship, family, or career. In writing about relationships for example, describe how they started and ended, and what, if anything, was traumatic. List what you learned from each relationship and what important decisions you made about yourself or others as a result of each relationship. Regardless of the biographical focus, describe your feelings and emotions related to that area. Include areas of challenge, difficulty, and hang-up. This more focused sketch allows you to take a deeper look into an area of your life that you may be struggling with or that is not working for you.

3. Make a list of any resentment you feel towards others and the nature of those resentments. List your grudges and injuries (perceived or real). List your fears. Basically, investigate the negative feelings and reactions that have hindered or consumed you. What are you attracting as a result of these negatives? This will help you identify the roots to your struggle with sin.

4. Make a list of specific wrongs that others have done to you. How did these events make you feel, how did they affect your life afterwards, and what part did you play within each situation? In the same way, be honest with yourself about how you may have wronged others. For example, who are you angry with and why? Then, describe what part you played in hurting that other person, directly or indirectly. The point here is to understand yourself – your trigger points, feelings, and emotions – as opposed to laying blame on others. The more we can identify our reactions that have been triggered by trying or harmful situations and interactions with people, the more we can identify what we may be using as a justification for sin as well as the more we can extend compassion towards ourselves.

5

THE SPIRIT OF LONELINESS

"Loneliness and the feeling of being unwanted is the most terrible poverty."

Mother Theresa

After the initial turmoil of separating from my second husband, I felt like I was doing okay at being a mother. I escorted my children to their lessons while at the same time juggling the start-up of my own law practice. Things seemed to be going well, and I was very proud of my kids.

While the children were in grade school, they listened to me and did what they were told. They got along well with their teachers and were enjoying their lives and various activities. Teachers reported that they were polite and well behaved. As a result, I concluded that I was a great parent. I had successfully imparted what I had been taught: to focus on school, look clean and neat every day, and be polite when spoken to.

Almost immediately after I was saved in 2001, I thought to myself that my kids would never be difficult teenagers and that our little family would skate through those years without any difficulty whatsoever. Now that Jesus was a part of my life, how could this not be so? I even recall saying to myself that, because of my excellent parenting skills and the fine home that I had provided for my children, they would never be "one of those kids" who got into drugs, alcohol, skipped school, or got involved in other undesirable activities that "other people's kids" engaged in.

Almost as soon as those thoughts arose, however, trouble descended. Without breaching the privacy of my children, let me just say that, for the next twelve years, we experienced a tsunami of difficulties: insolence, insubordination, drug and alcohol abuse, non-completion of high school, involvement with the criminal justice system, youth detention, and on a couple of occasions, aggressive behavior towards me. It was truly a mentally, emotionally, and physically exhausting time for everyone.

I cried many times thinking that my little family was coming apart at the seams and would never be whole. I worried constantly about my kids, wondering if they would ever overcome their inner demons or simply lose themselves completely to the darkness that enveloped them. I was continuously anxious for their safety and felt the deep hurt of witnessing them step onto paths of self-destruction and feeling helpless on the sidelines.

I was wounded, too, by how my own flesh and blood could turn on me. At times, I was treated with varying degrees of disrespect all the way through to outright abusiveness. I felt guilty, believing that my divorce from their father was the root cause of all this trouble.

What I now realize is, like my parents before me, that I had not established a listening and compassionate ear towards my children. I had neglected to create a safe connection for them to come to me with whatever they were facing. Instead, I had been focused entirely on outward appearances instead of inward realities. Although I have never inquired of my children, I suspect that they felt much like I did at their age – lonely for a deep, authentic relationship with their parent. In my unhealed state, I had been unable to give to my children what I had yearned for as a teenager...and a cycle perpetuated itself.

During that multi-year odyssey of chaos, still unmarried without any prospects on the horizon, another married man appeared. In my state of battle fatigue, this man looked like he could offer a bit of tangible, emotional shelter from the storm raging around me. I was tired of being alone, worn out from my single-handed battle with teenagers, and was very frustrated that I was not married. I allowed my unresolved loneliness to drive my decision to get involved with yet another married man.

To be honest, I was also feeling angry with God. I considered what I perceived to be His continued refusal to bring me a husband, one who could be my helpmeet in parenting, as the reason I was having all these difficulties with my children. Permitting my anger to turn into rebellion, I turned my back on God. Once again, I deliberately opened the door to sin. I knew what I was doing wrong on every level, but I decided not to care about the consequences.

I used my loneliness to justify rebellion against God's laws.

Recently, I was one of about 15 speakers at a conference for Christian business leaders. At the end of the day, some of us were asked to sit on a panel to discuss a variety of topics. The final question put to us was, *"What do you do when you feel lonely?"*

The answers were as varied as the speakers. Some said they would spend time with loved ones or their business partners. Others said they would fellowship with God by reading the Word when they felt lonely.

However, one speaker said something that really hit me. He said, *"I never get lonely. I have the Holy Spirit living inside of me, so I am never lonely. And if I ever feel like I am about to be lonely, I read the Scriptures that remind me that Jesus will never leave me nor forsake me. I take hold of these Scriptures until the feeling of loneliness passes."*

In that moment, I realized the obvious: *I was without excuse!*

The idea of taking hold of Scriptures until loneliness dissipated caused me to stop in my tracks and give myself a reality check. Why had I not remembered to take hold of Scripture when I knew perfectly well that God's Word is both a shield and a sword against Satan? It's not like I didn't know that, so what was really going on? I was challenged to look deeper still within myself to the place where I could admit that something even more disturbing was contributing to my loneliness.

Despite my sincere confession of faith and my leaning on my brothers and sisters in Christ for prayer and support during my children's terrible, teenage years, I simply did not believe what God says in His Word.

The heart is deceitful above all things, and desperately sick; who can understand it?
~ Jeremiah 17:9

The pull of the flesh – of wickedness or sin – on the heart was a concept for others, not for me. In reality, what did I really know about my own heart? I knew only what pain, unhappiness, and loneliness felt like. I refused to face the fact that I had given myself over to selfish and worldly things. I was behaving like I didn't understand that I, like all humanity, have a leaning toward sin because of the fall of Adam and Eve in the garden. Because of deceitfulness, my heart tricked me into believing myself incapable of committing any sin.

"Wicked" and "deceitful" were words I would have never described myself with. Although saved and considered one of the righteous by God's Grace, pride had blinded me from the truth that I was a redeemed child of God in constant need of a Savior *especially* as a believer. I was a believer who struggled with sin habits with the tendency to indulge in selfishness at the expense of my relationship with God.

The crack through which I allowed the enemy to enter was my loneliness. He blinded me to the effects a deceitful heart can have when one is not fully yielded to the Lord. Because I did not believe what God said in His Word about who I was in Christ and how He was there to help me live uprightly, I gave my heart over to selfish desires and the deceptions of the enemy.

When I fail to abide in Christ, I am rejecting the One in whom I am able find comfort and companionship. When I choose, instead, to give myself over to feeling lonely, I fail to take hold of (meditate on and believe) Scriptures that refute the notion that I am alone. When I forget through pride that my heart can be deceived, I become easy pickings for Satan. I have found it is easier to be deceived when I have neglected to fill my mind and heart with the Word of God or to pray for protection from the enemy. Satan is always ready to exploit my own base desires and selfishness. Reading and applying God's Word – abiding in Christ – is a necessity, without which, I am at risk of walking in sin again.

Within every believer there exists a tension. This tension is between the natural and the spiritual, the flesh (one's worldly desires and sin habits) and the spirit and that which is imparted of God. This life-long tug-of-war is something that all believers, I included, must contend with on a daily basis.

As the Bible clearly states, I must daily surrender my thoughts, will, pride, heart, and imaginations to the only One who can cut out both the dandelion and the entire root system: Jesus. It is only through Jesus that I can completely get rid of old sin habits. It is only through Jesus that I can be changed.

The apostle Paul stated it best:

Do not be conformed to this world, but be transformed by the renewal of your mind, that by testing you may discern what is the will of God, what is good and acceptable and perfect.
~Romans 12:2

Abiding in Christ means that I am allowing the Spirit to transform my mind. With the right thought patterns being replaced by the Lord, I can then resist the enemy and how he can deceive my heart. My discernment increases, and I am able to successfully walk in the will of God.

Jesus says in His Word that, in our anger, we must not sin.[7] Because of what I have gone through and experienced, I would add that in times of loneliness, we must not sin. When loneliness sets in, we need to take hold of Scriptures like Deuteronomy 31:8 that states that, *"It is the Lord who goes before you. He will be with you: he will not leave you or forsake you. Do not fear or be dismayed."* We must choose to believe the Word versus giving into our loneliness and having it lead to sin.

Loneliness, like anger, is an emotion that can distract you from focusing on the Savior. Without that focus, we can be led down paths of sin. Our emotions are not wrong, but if not dealt with properly and brought to the feet of Jesus, they can turn into a breeding ground for sin to take root.

---

[7] See Ephesians 4:26

In the last chapter, we spent some time excavating "family of origin" issues. We also spent time recording who we really are, what hurts us, and what causes us pain. This is not light work and can be really heavy slogging. If you feel exhausted from that work, I ask that Jesus comfort and strengthen you. He is right there with you, an ever-present help in times of trouble[8].

I pray that my story of loneliness and rebellion has stirred within you the need to examine a particular area in your life that may be causing you to stumble. Don't be afraid to investigate how different root causes (such as loneliness) can affect your life. Remember always that there is hope in Jesus. By meditating on Scripture and making the choice to believe what God says, you can uproot those things that are wreaking havoc in your life.

---

[8] See Psalm 46:1

Let's Pray:

Thank you, God, that You are Sovereign and that You see all and know all. Please open the eyes of my heart to myself as well as to any deception I may be under. Please show me what I need to see about myself right now, and give me Your strength to be honest about my life and the sin I am walking in. Please wake me up, Lord, so that I can clearly see what I am doing that is dishonouring to You and harmful to me. I declare that I can do all things through Christ Jesus, including this task.[9] Thank you, Father. In Jesus' Name. Amen.

Reflection – Stop and Assess the Situation

Take out your journal again and record your honest answers to the following questions:

1. Are you still carrying around any unresolved hurt, pain, loneliness, or anger from the past? If so, write about it now.

---

[9] See Philippians 4:13

2. What in your past has created a need or a void in you that you may be using to justify sin? What is the nature of that void? How was or is your sin supposed to fulfill those needs or void?

3. Write out your justification for sin. Are you justifying or rationalizing any sinful actions because of unresolved pride, hurt, pain, anger, loneliness, or low self-esteem, etc.? The more you flesh out your rationalizations, the more you will help yourself. Don't judge your answers, because if you do, you won't be honest. Just record your answers like an investigative journalist objectively records the facts.

6

COMPASSION OF JESUS

*For now we see in a mirror dimly,
but then face to face.
Now I know in part; then I shall know fully,
even as I have been fully known.*

1 Corinthians 13:12

Sometime after my relationship with the last married man dissolved and I began releasing him from my heart, God brought a single, Christian man into my life, a man that I thought at the time was the God-given helpmeet that I had long prayed for. This man, whom I shall call Alex,[10] was a man who had endured severe trials and difficulties throughout his own life. These trials were of a kind that would have crushed a normal person and, in fact, drove him to plan for his own demise. His plans, however, were

---

[10] Name changed to protect privacy

interrupted by Jesus who saved him from both his spiritual and physical death, leaving him with an uncommon gentleness and concern for those suffering from similar difficulties.

I was drawn in like bears to honey.

As I learned more about Alex, I discovered that the darkness and life-altering experiences he had endured were offset by his professional success. Despite the chaos in his life, his energy to accomplish great things was impressive. He definitely possessed something that attracted me to him.

Part of the attraction was that, in many ways, I recognized myself in him. He, also, had been raised within an environment of perfectionism and had learned to "do" rather than to "be". He had been abandoned emotionally as a young child, often hearing from his father to stop crying and be a man. Like me, Alex had learned to stuff down his emotions, living his life in a constant state of feeling rejected and unloved although that was likely not the reality. Whereas I had used my relationships with men to fill the void, substance abuse became his antidote to the pain he felt within. Our similar upbringings and struggles certainly influenced our connection.

It felt like God had drawn us together. Alex was like a mirror that I could gaze into and see myself clearly, thus erasing the loneliness I felt. In turn, I believed I was to bring to him unconditional love and tenderness to help him move on from his past and how he had defined himself. It appeared that we had a perfectly beneficial relationship.

During our relationship, I was often surprised at how God softened my heart towards Alex when he would do or say something that was unfamiliar to my normal way of being. Instead, I found myself responding to Alex with love and compassion despite my strong predisposition to judge. As I would listen to his story about his life, a life that my family of origin would never have been able to understand let alone have any compassion for, my heart felt tender towards him.

I discovered that being judgmental builds relationship walls. These walls come between the one we are judging and ourselves. These walls stop us from entering the door of trust and into their deepest places of sorrow where compassion is most needed and desired.

Judgment emotionally isolates us from ourselves and from community with others.

I admired as well as envied Alex's ability to hear from the Holy Spirit. As he gently challenged my thoughts and feelings, it seemed as if he could see right through me, catching me off guard many times. He was continually prompting me to take more responsibility for my feelings instead of blaming others.

On one occasion, Alex said something that I took offence to. His exact words escape my recall, but the message that I heard felt like rejection. Because I was not good at expressing my needs in a non-manipulative way, I said nothing, fearing that Alex would leave me. I was stuck in that terrible yet familiar place of needing to speak my truth but fearing that if I did, rejection would surely follow.

Alex watched as my silence betrayed me. He very quietly asked me whether we were going to talk about what was going on. This, too, was new for me, as my childhood experiences with having messy emotions were met with a demand to stop sulking and to put a smile on my face. These demands led to the conclusion that there was something wrong with honestly expressing myself. Nevertheless, instead of just putting up with my silent treatment, Alex quietly persevered. He kept inviting me to try and tell him what was going on in my heart.

Above all, keep loving one another earnestly, since love covers a multitude of sins.
~ 1 Peter 4:8

Demonstrating some tough love, Alex pointed out that I was playing the victim, something no one had ever accused me of before. Initially, I vehemently rejected that assertion. Some days later, however, God had me sit quietly and receive that revelation deep into my spirit. Finally, I understood the root of my problem.

The reason I had never learned to accept and express my feelings was for fear of being rejected for doing so. My upbringing of having to suppress my emotions and, as a result, not learning to express them healthfully had contributed to my reluctance to share from the heart. In addition, I had taken my perceptions of emotional abandonment as a young child into each relationship with a man, controlling and manipulating what I said or didn't say, all in an effort to thwart rejection.

Alex was now inviting me to step out from behind my fears and habits and enter into the uncharted territory of emotional honesty. When he asked me if I wanted to be delivered from this, I thought about it and said yes. Alex quietly prayed for me, asking God to take this from me and to heal me from the fear of rejection and of playing the victim. Without even a hint of condemnation,

Alex's prayers, spoken with his quiet, reassuring voice, opened the door for healing into my deep and scarred places of brokenness.

I really appreciated Alex. He had an uncommon and deep trust in God, never wanting to make a move without hearing from the Holy Spirit. He knew from his own experiences that his "self" could and would lead him astray every time. His consistent faithfulness in this area served to highlight how infrequently I had been seeking God's direction on things, both big and small. Through Alex, I learned that God must come first in all my decisions. Rather than being an afterthought, I needed to make Him my first point of contact in all things. Teaching by example, Alex encouraged me to surrender myself daily to God lest my ego or broken heart rise up to rule and create havoc in my life. Furthermore, I could trust Him, too.

For the first time in my life, I was in a relationship that I believed was from God. I was excited to think that perhaps I had been blessed with a man that I could build a life with for our mutual benefit and for the furtherance of the Kingdom. Perhaps the mate that I had been asking God for had finally arrived.

About eleven months into the relationship, however, things began shifting into a familiar and unwanted place. Something was happening with Alex that I could neither understand nor control. He began disconnecting from me like a light bulb dimming during a brownout, until one night, he announced that we needed to "take a break". I had seen it coming but was trying desperately not to notice.

Still battling self-doubt, my immediate reaction was to ask Alex what I had done or said to cause him to disengage. He assured me it had nothing to do with me but had everything to do with him…and I took him at his word. Alex was not a man who lied or said whatever someone else wanted to hear. Yet, when I looked into his eyes, instead of seeing a clear truth, all I saw was a dark emptiness that saddened me.

I couldn't understand what was happening with Alex. My spirit told me that it was not good, like maybe his past had come back and grabbed hold of him somehow. Or perhaps, Alex was unable to receive a love that forced him to admit that he was worthy of being loved just as he was. Despite his apparent closeness with God, he was struggling with something. Whatever it was, I was hurt by his withdrawal and, for a time, this felt unforgiveable.

In that terrible moment when a long-desired relationship ends, emotions become raw, causing acute pain so fierce that we are often unable to see things from the other's perspective. The drawbridge to our heart pulls up, and we retreat behind our walls to tend our wounds and harbour our anger. So it was with me.

I was confused and fiercely angry with Alex. I had desperately wanted our relationship to be what I had hoped and prayed for. In hurt and anger, I lashed out with an abusive email that I regretted as soon as I pressed send. I kept replaying the question in my mind of *"Why would he do that to me?"*

One of my immediate reactions was to angrily ask God why He had allowed this relationship to dissolve. Nothing made any sense to me. Furthermore, I responded by doing what I always did when things went wrong. I decided I needed to get away from it all.

Running away to get away from the pain is, of course, fruitless. When we are harbouring pain, it dwells inside of us whether we are at home or away. So when I arrived at that beautiful resort deep in the mountains, I tried to put on a brave face, a common trick that fooled everyone except me. I was neither brave nor happy.

My dreams were in tatters upon the rocks. I was intensely sad and disappointed. It felt like my life was in ruins once again.

In desperation, I called Alex and asked him to join me at the resort, even though I knew he did not want to be with me. Once again, I was prepared to hide behind my defenses in order to not feel rejected and alone. I wanted him to want me, but I was already building walls around my heart.

Alex thought and prayed about it. In the end, he refused my invitation explaining that he felt like God had something for me that would only be imparted to me if I were alone at that resort.

At that moment, I didn't want what God had for me. I wanted Alex...and I wanted our relationship to be what it used to be. I wanted the here and now, not the unseen and the maybe.

Settling into my lovely cabin, I gazed at God's gorgeous creation laid out before me outside my window. I wondered how I would survive three days of being alone with myself. No longer able to hold back the tears, I cried aloud in my misery to God for what I felt was the most significant reality of the situation: *"He doesn't want me! Alex doesn't want me!"*

As I comprehended what I knew to be the truth, life-long feelings of despair, rejection, and pain that I thought were long gone and resolved overwhelmed me.

The only relationship that I had believed God had ordained and that I thought would be my last had gone to waste. I was alone again.

Consumed with that terrible, well-known feeling of rejection, I was transported back to my teenage years and to every failed relationship that seemed to define my life. A familiar refrain echoed in my head, *"I am not worthy of a man's forever love."* I sat in that beautiful, resort room in the midst of God's perfection believing that once again, I had taken a risk at love and had gotten kicked in the teeth.

For several minutes, I cried in my loneliness and desperation. Slowly and quietly though, as if my tears and despair were a Heavenly invitation, I felt the Holy Spirit's presence in my heart. Calmness enveloped me, and I was led to open the Gideon Bible at the bedside to Song of Solomon. I began reading each line very, very slowly. I was glued to the words on the page and could not have averted my attention even if I had wanted to.

I continued to read until I arrived at Chapter 2, verse 10 when I was arrested by its words, and I ended up reading it repeatedly.

My beloved speaks and says to me:
"Arise, my love, my beautiful one,
and come away."

As I read these words over and over, the impact of that message began to sink in. The truth of God's Word written in that beautiful love song rose slowly inside of me. I heard myself quietly say through tears, *"Jesus, You want me! You want me!"*

Through my absolute despair and brokenness, Jesus gently appeared as my Rescuer. His outstretched hand invited me to come away with Him, the one person who would never reject or forsake me. An inner joy quietly bubbled up as I realized that I was totally loved and accepted by Him.

The compassion of Jesus enveloped me!

In that moment, I wondered whether Jesus had allowed this entire situation with Alex, a situation that had unfortunately included pain and disappointment. Working it for my good, God used this pain and disappointment to lead me to the place of recognizing that my desperate, broken, and empty self needed Him...and *only* Him. In reaching the absolute end of myself, He orchestrated it so that I would have no choice but to allow Him to take His rightful place of prominence in *every* nook and cranny of my heart.

Jesus revealed that, despite my handing over all other aspects and circumstances of my life to Him, I had never really given Him my whole heart. I had overlooked Him as the one, true lover of my soul. He was my Beloved and the One for whom I had waited and hoped for all my life. He now beckoned me to me arise and come away with Him.

My brokenness and suffering created a vacuum into which Jesus quietly crept, filling every empty space in my heart like water fills in a jar full of pebbles. Jesus saw me in my childlike weakness and pain and desired me nonetheless. He loved me *for me* rather than for what I could accomplish, how smart I was, or how perfect I presented myself as. He pursued me with His extravagant love and devotion despite my sin, imperfections, failures, rebellion, and even my rejection of Him as a believer.

What kind of Savior is this who pursues those who reject Him, even those who confess their allegiance to Him?

In that moment, I realized that Jesus not only sees me as I am, but fully knows me as the Scriptures promise. I am fully known by Jesus and yet fully pursued by Him. Despite my serious character flaws, sexual immorality, emotional dishonesty, fear, victim-mentality, anger, hard-heartedness, pride, and rebellion, Jesus knows me fully and pursues me relentlessly anyway. I am worthy of His love despite all my shortcomings, hidden or otherwise.

God showed me something else even more important.

Once we receive God's unconditional love and acceptance and have a revelation of what this means, we are faced with the terrible knowledge that the people in our lives, the ones who we trusted to love us perfectly, in fact, did not. We have all been let down by our primary caregivers no matter how wonderful they might have been. We have all had unmet expectations in close relationships, yet it is not the other person's fault. *Mere humans cannot love us perfectly as God does.* To expect them to do so is nothing short of madness. Yet, it is a tough truth that we must digest nonetheless.

Then we must choose.

Our choice is to either forgive those who have failed us...or not forgive them. In order to make the right choice, we must understand that our parents and others who we have been in relationship with were (and are) incapable of showing that perfect, vast, and supernatural love that only God can provide. Then, we must comprehend the consequences of our choice to forgive them or not. This is a choice that ultimately leads us to either life or death.

I knew what I needed to do. I could no longer make excuses. I needed to forgive Alex.

Even though I knew that forgiveness is a gift that I give myself, my heart was hurting too much. To be honest, I did not *want* to forgive. I wanted to stay in the blame-game, the "I hate you, Alex" game.

Scripture does not tell us to forgive only when we feel like it. It simply tells us to forgive. As we read in Colossians 3:13, we are to *"forgive as the Lord forgave [us]."*

Some of us have to repeatedly ask the Holy Spirit to help us forgive those who have hurt us. We simply cannot do it in our own strength. After all, unforgiveness serves a purpose that satisfies our selfish desires. It affords us the "right" to stay in judgment and blame others for all the bad things in our lives, including that which is of our own making. Thus, it is an entry point into which Satan will creep and wreak havoc in our lives.

I knew that I absolutely needed to forgive. Choosing to forgive would enable me to move on and be clear and clean of any iniquity or "sludge" in my heart. This sludge was making me ill, foggy-brained, and hard-hearted. Also, if I truly desired to live a life in the contentedness of God's presence and in the ease of His will, I had to forgive.

The need to forgive goes deeper still.

Should we decide *not* to forgive others, we become like the wicked servant whose enormous debt to his master was forgiven. The servant then refused to forgive a much smaller debt owed to him from someone else. In Matthew 18:34, we read that the master became enraged and delivered the servant to the jailers *to be tortured* until he could pay all his debt.

Unforgiveness comes at a terrible price: spiritual torture and absence from the Holy of Holies. In addition, unforgiveness traps us into feeling entitled into not loving ourselves or loving others. In the end, we become a slave to the sin of unforgiveness.

My breakup with Alex, as painful as it was, led me to recognize my own brokenness, a brokenness that only Jesus could heal. I subsequently realized that, up until then, I had reserved my heart for a mere man, expecting him to love and fill me in a way that only Jesus can. In that pivotal moment in that mountain cabin, Jesus touched me as no one else could, breathing into me a love and acceptance that began to permeate the deep recesses of my broken heart. Through His healing touch, compassion, and grace, I was able to forgive Alex for the hurt that he'd caused me. God took a bad situation and turned it around for my good.

Let's Pray:

Holy Spirit, please help us to discern why terrible things happen to us, and especially how You can turn them around and use them for our growth and refinement. Please help us to remain calm and contented in You in the midst of our trials and hurts, knowing that our pain and disappointment has a multi-faceted purpose for our good although we may not see it at the time.

Please help us to surrender, not only our circumstances, but also our whole heart to You. Help us to forgive those who have hurt us as well as ourselves so that we may continue to enjoy Your presence and guidance in everything we say and do.

We admit our dependence upon You to soften our heart when it is hard and unforgiving. Thank you for helping us to ask for Your blessing upon those who have hurt us[11] as Your Word requires.

Thank you that You can change our hearts into what You desire them to be. Thank you also that You see us for who we are, for our failures and faithlessness, and yet You fully know us, desire us, and pursue us for Your purposes. Amen.

---

[11] See Luke 6:28 & Matthew 5:44

7

INTO THE LIGHT

*"There are those who are clean
in their own eyes
but are not washed of their filth."*

Proverbs 30:12

In many ways, Alex had been like a security agent at the airport within our relationship. I'm talking about the agents that direct you into one of the security lines where you and your bags are x-rayed, exposing everything you thought was hidden. This relationship had funneled me to a place where my inner baggage of deep brokenness was exposed.

I was led to resolutely look into that dark and foreboding room in my heart where I had hidden my perfectionism, self-judgment, and fear of rejection. In fact, I had hidden them so well that I had no idea they were there.

When I fearfully examined that dark place in my heart, I found it occupied by a shadowy figure.

A closer inspection revealed that it was the person of Jesus sitting quietly in that lonely and dark place. He was waiting for me – for *me* – to enter in and fellowship with Him again. Close fellowship, however, was not all that He desired. He wanted my complete rejection of sin and a wholehearted return to Him. He yearned to show Himself to me yet again in all His righteousness...and that this righteousness was mine because of Jesus.

As a believer, my walk has at times been very wobbly. My instability of faith was due entirely to my not being disciplined to stay in the Word, seek after God, and pray. In some seasons, I have been fully committed to God. In other seasons, I have distanced myself from Him, even backslid into doing my own thing, rejecting His principles. Meanwhile, Jesus stood watching and loving me in His most excellent and perfect way, waiting patiently for me to once again throw up the white flag of surrender.

Despite my faithless "to-ing" and "fro-ing", Jesus remained steadfast. His character was and is completely and utterly constant. He always will be the definition of reliable. He is like a lighthouse beacon in our lives, keeping us from crashing on the rocks. He will point the way to safe and calm waters if we let Him.

The light of Jesus is so bright and all encompassing that we can stand face-to-face with Him and the backside of us is illuminated also. His light and Spirit is all revealing and all surrounding. Nothing is hidden from it. It is terrible and wonderful all at the same time.

In that mountain resort when I again came face-to-face with Jesus, He spoke to me about surrendering to Him *all* of my heart. Very specifically, He convicted me of my deliberate and self-serving actions of having affairs with married men. Jesus saw the sexual sin that I had engaged in as a believer, and it grieved Him. Yet, instead of rejecting me, He invited me to turn from my sinful ways, exchanging my selfishness for His righteousness.

He had a plan for my life that was frustrated by my sin.

Next, God brought to my remembrance the story of the prodigal son who decided to return home after wasting his money and time on fleshly desires. As he headed home to make amends with his father, the Bible says that the father ran towards the son *"while he was still a long way off"*[12] with a heart full of compassion. He was ecstatic that his son had returned.

It is so easy to believe that, once we step across enemy lines and commit sin, God will refuse to accept us back into the fold. Many believe that our sins can totally and forever ruin our place in God's family. This is neither true nor biblical. If we are to be restored, we must do our part: we must turn away and repent of our sin. With that decision made, we need to head back towards our home with the Father just as the prodigal son did.

I must walk the path of obedience and submission to God and His ways and

---

[12] Read the Parable of the Prodigal Son – Luke 15:11-24

commands. It is when I walk that path that God sees me from a long way off and comes running to meet me. As a gentleman and one who honours the gift of free will that He has granted all of humanity, He will not force me to return to Him. However, He will always be ready to forgive me and receive me back into fellowship with Him.

It was in recognizing my immoral behaviour and insubordination towards God that my heart broke as it did on the day I gave my heart to the Lord. My contrite and repentant heart shattered anew for I had again thrust the spear into His side, grieving Him afresh with my backslidden ways. As He did in the first hour that I believed, He was again faithful to pour out upon me His healing oil of grace and forgiveness.

Being in His presence and receiving His conviction, correction, forgiveness, healing, and cleansing is more comforting and lovely than anything this world has to offer.

In that cabin deep in the stillness of God's magnificent creation, Jesus led me to a profound understanding that I had once embraced but had since forsaken. King David said it best:

Against you, you only, have I sinned and done what is evil in your sight, so that you may be justified in your words and blameless in your judgment.
~ Psalm 51:4

Busted!

Sin, as defined in the Bible, is a vertical assault against God. I had assaulted God when I crossed into forbidden territory and gotten involved with married men. I had sinned against God and done evil in His sight. It is an understatement to say that these are sobering words. Frankly, I thank God that He brought me to such a deep, jarring awareness of the depth of my immoral habit and the toll it was taking on my relationship with Him.

I am constantly amazed at the truths that I read in the Bible. These truths settle in my spirit like a gear dropping into place, resonating with every fiber of my being. God's Word proves what is right and wrong, leading those who believe to Truth that convicts and leads to repentance.

A few months after Alex and I went our separate ways, God brought to my attention a book that gave me even more insight into my betrayal of God and His principles and commands. The subject of this book was not foreign to me having listened to plenty of sermons on the topic before. To my detriment, I had never really given the subject matter my persistent and urgent attention. Now, I was compelled to study this text as though my life depended on it.

The subject was spiritual warfare. God used the book called *The Invisible War: What Every Believer Needs to Know about Satan, Demons, and Spiritual Warfare* by Chip Ingram to teach me. Before reading Mr. Ingram's book, my view of Satan was only that he existed and was real. However, I did not pay too much attention to him. Although

I ascribed much of what went on with my children as the tampering of Satan, I somehow did not make the connection between my own loneliness and the operations of the enemy.

I did not understand that Satan used my loneliness to keep me focused on my own problems instead of on God. The enemy whispered in my ear, manipulating me by saying, *"Did God really say that He would never leave you nor forsake you?"* and *"Go ahead. You deserve this."* I was blind to how subtle Satan can be, or how he can get into our thought life with the stealth of a jewel thief. Satan is like a virus in a computer. He silently invades and corrupts the operating system without any forewarning until the entire system is spitting out nonsense, incapable of functioning the way it was designed to.

Getting a good grasp on the plans, purposes, and methods of Satan has helped me understand myself in a whole new light. It has opened my eyes to the deceptions of the enemy, allowing me to call myself out on my own relational recklessness. I now see Satan for what he is – the ultimate terrorist who seeks to destroy God's people and God's programs as Ingram describes it.

Ingram goes on to say that Satan's objective is to discourage, deceive, divide, and destroy. He is the personal and corporate enemy of God's people and programs. As believers, we must understand how Satan works. Yet, we must never fear him, for he is a defeated foe because of Christ's work on the cross.

Satan hates it when believers focus on God, pray, and read His Word. The enemy hates God and knows that He is all-powerful. Furthermore, Satan knows that he was defeated on the cross of Calvary…so he gets back at God through His children.

Satan works hard to get us to doubt God and His plans for us. He wants us to do exactly what Adam and Eve did – thumb our collective noses at His commands and precepts. Through believing the enemy's lies, we trust in our own wisdom. As a result, we think that we are entitled to commit whatever act we are contemplating because we are under the false belief that it is somehow for our own benefit.

Satan's agenda includes manipulating us into ignoring God and declaring our independence from Him. Having believers fall away from relationship with their Lord and Savior and coming to ruin is his delight. It makes his day when he can get us to destroy our own testimony and forsake God by walking in sin, as I did. His mission is to knock us off our feet and off the course that God has set out for us, bringing to nothing the plans and purposes He has for each one of us. Our destruction is his ultimate goal.

We must understand that we humans are not merely the spoils of the heavenly war. Humans *are* the battlefield in the war between God and Satan. We must also realize that despite the fact that Satan has no power to overthrow God and His Kingdom, he will continue to press in against us. His ego is so out of control he will continue to attack us even though he has no authority against a saved believer. He has no authority, that is, unless we give in to him.

Therefore, we must understand our foe and be vigilantly aware of the ways and means he employs to get us to take our focus off God, His commands, and His vision for us. The more we know and understand Satan's plans and tactics, the easier and faster it will be for us to defeat his attempts to destroy us.

Let us take another look at an old story in the next chapter that will help us understand our enemy and how he operates. This, in turn, will help us understand ourselves as well.

8

ENEMY AT THE GATE

The creation story tells how God created the earth, sky, stars, seas, wildlife, and vegetation in five days. Then on the sixth day, He created man for a stated purpose:

Then God said, "Let us make man in our image, after our likeness. And let them have dominion over the fish of the sea and over the birds of the heavens and over the livestock and over all the earth and over every creeping thing that creeps on the earth."
~ Genesis 1:26

Like a potter labors with love over a formless lump of clay, shaping it into the beautiful, finished product he or she envisions, God created man by forming dust together. God intended that man should not only tend His wondrous creation, but he should also enjoy its bounty and provision. God's plan for man was perfect – a complete and unabridged unity between God and man along with complete and perfect provision from the earth's bounty. Original man needed nothing else. God did not just create man from a fresh and unique prototype. He created man *"in His own image"*[13] and *"likeness"*. This is a profound mystery and one that we all need to sit quietly and seek God's revelation on.

Man (men and women alike) was made in God's *image and likeness.* If we are not sure what that *image* looks like, we have only to look at Jesus.

He is the image of the invisible God, the firstborn of all creation.
~ Colossians 1:15

We were made to bear the likeness of God – to be holy, sinless, and righteous. Looking at the person and life of Jesus gives us a very clear picture of how we were made, what God intended for us, and how we are to think and act and connect with God.

---

[13] Genesis 1:27

It is important to note, however, that while we were made to be *like* God and *made in His image*, we were never made to *be* God.

We all know the story. God created Adam and then placed him in the beautiful and serene Garden of Eden that contained two special trees: the Tree of Life and the Tree of Knowledge of Good and Evil. God's inaugural and irrevocable royal edict to Adam was:

And the Lord God commanded the man, saying, "You may surely eat of every tree of the garden, but of the tree of the knowledge of good and evil you shall not eat, for in the day that you eat of it you shall surely die."
~ Genesis 2:16-17

After God gave Adam his first and most important instructions, He created Eve as a special companion and helpmeet for Adam. And God was very pleased with all that He had created.

We discover in Scripture that Satan, who was once an angel, was cast out of Heaven with a third of the angels for inciting a rebellion against God. We read about Satan's motivation for challenging God in Isaiah 14:13-14:

You said in your heart, "I will ascend to heaven; above the stars of God I will set my throne on high; I will sit on the mount of assembly in the far reaches of the north; I will ascend above the heights of the clouds; I will make myself like the Most High."

Satan has had an axe to grind with God from the beginning. What better way to get back at God than to tamper with His created beings that He put in charge of the whole of creation. All the while, Satan's goal was to become like God and to trick those made in His image to follow him and not God.

Capable of changing himself into any form he wanted to, Satan took on the form of a snake. Described in Genesis 3:1 as *"more crafty than any other beast of the field that the Lord God had made",* Satan approached Eve seeking revenge upon God for kicking him out of paradise. Satan's aim was to ruin God's intended purpose for His beloved, created mankind.

I find it interesting that Eve received Satan so easily and readily. She seemed neither fearful nor skeptical. Instead, she welcomed him willingly. No doubt, he appeared like a credible messenger from heaven with what Eve must have perceived as a helpful and valuable plan that she could gain something from.

Oh, how crafty Satan is.

Satan could have asked God to revoke His royal decree and tell His created beings that He had changed His mind, and that it was okay for them to eat from the forbidden tree. Satan knew, however, that God would never change His royal laws, rules, and commands. He certainly would never take orders from Satan, the fallen and rebellious former angel with aspirations to usurp the Most High God.

Satan also could have approached Eve head-on and pushed as to why she should believe that God had told her not to eat from the forbidden tree. That head-on approach was too risky though. Eve could have defended the edict all the more with such an obvious "attack".

No. I believe that Satan knew that his only hope of getting Adam and Eve to declare independence from God was to get Eve to decide *in her own mind* to disobey God. He understood that his success depended on whether humankind could rationalize or give reasons for their departure from "doing it God's way". To pull off his plan to get Eve to self-deceive, Satan employed a subtle and crafty approach to sow doubt into her mind about what God had commanded.

"Did God actually say, 'You shall not eat of any tree in the garden'?"
~ Genesis 3:1b

Eve didn't fall for it. She corrected Satan (although she got the instruction slightly wrong) demonstrating that she knew what the rule was. She relayed that God allowed them to eat from the trees in the garden except the tree in the middle of the garden and that if they even *touched* the tree they *would surely die.*

Not giving up, Satan changed his approach. He replied with two lies and a temptation.

..."You will not surely die. For God knows that when you eat of it your eyes will be opened, and you will be like God, knowing good and evil."
~ Genesis 3:4-5

Satan attempted to convince Eve that God had lied to her about the consequences of eating the fruit. He planted the seed that He was withholding something good with His command. Twisting the truth (for her eyes *were* opened in the end), he made it appear like a better result was to be achieved by going against God's "ridiculous" and "restrictive" laws.

Do not miss this point.

Satan's primary method is to get us to believe that God has told us nothing but lies and that God and His Word are not to be believed or trusted. Even I have been plagued with those thoughts periodically. All believers will have to face the doubts that the enemy tries to throw at them.

Satan argued that by disobeying God (eating the fruit), Eve would gain a benefit that far outweighed the disadvantage of disobedience. This temptation secured in Eve's mind the thought that she was in a better position than God to decide what was best for her life. It is like saying that a car knows better than its inventor how to keep itself running in peak condition.

Satan's attack was diabolical. He caused Eve to doubt herself (as God had created her) and then doubt God and His plans for her. Being full of doubt about God and emboldened by the promise of Satan's lie that she would become like God if she ate the forbidden fruit, Eve took the bait. She convinced herself that the created thing (fruit) was more desirable than the Creator.

So when the woman saw that the tree was good for food, and that it was a delight to the eyes, and that the tree was to be desired to make one wise, she took of its fruit and ate...
~ Genesis 3:6a

And thus, a pattern was set for mankind. This pattern is to doubt God as our ultimate authority, to doubt that God knows best for His created beings, and to make an idol of His creation instead of worshipping the Creator God. This set in motion the pull of the flesh – doing things in a worldly way with a limited human understanding – against the pull of the spirit – doing things God's way with the trust that His intentions and commands are superior and wiser.

Next, Eve tempted Adam with the same forbidden fruit. He, too, ate of the fruit, choosing to go against God's command.

...and she also gave some to her husband who was with her, and he ate.
~ Genesis 3:6b

This Scripture highlights another point we must not miss. Adam was standing *with Eve* throughout her conversation with the serpent, listening to the entire conversation. Adam knew what the rules were regarding the tree in the middle of the Garden, so why did he just stand there and let Eve disobey God? Why didn't he jump in and protect his wife against the wiles of Satan? Why didn't he defend God's laws and stand up for truth in a way that may have convinced Eve to think twice about her actions and resist the serpent's wiles? Adam too was seduced by Satan's lie that he (Adam) would become *like God* if he ate the fruit.

Adam and Eve wanted to make their own decisions apart from any authority. They decided that declaring their independence from God took precedence over being obedient to Him. They fed their flesh, their pride, and their ego at the expense of their coveted, symbiotic, perfect existence with God in the Garden of Eden. And in that moment, Satan became the rogue authority on the earth, a position that he was never legally appointed to hold.

Satan arrogantly tempted Jesus in the wilderness in the same way.

Then Jesus was led up by the Spirit into the wilderness to be tempted by the devil. And after fasting forty days and forty nights, he was hungry. And the tempter came and said to him, "If you are the Son of God, command these stones to become loaves of bread." But he answered, "It is written,

*"'Man shall not live by bread alone,
but by every word that comes
from the mouth of God.'"*

Then the devil took him to the holy city and set him on the pinnacle of the temple and said to him, "If you are the Son of God, throw yourself down, for it is written,

"'He will command his angels concerning you,'

and

*"'On their hands they will bear you up,
lest you strike your foot against a stone.'"*

Jesus said to him, "Again it is written, 'You shall not put the Lord your God to the test.'" Again, the devil took him to a very high mountain and showed him all the kingdoms of the world and their glory. And he said to him, "All these I will give you, if you will fall down and worship me." Then Jesus said to him, "Be

gone, Satan! For it is written,
"'You shall worship the Lord your God
and him only shall you serve.'"
Then the devil left him, and behold, angels came and were ministering to him.
~ Matthew 4:1-11

The devil appealed to Jesus' flesh, pride, and ego with all that he promised and tempted Him to do. It's the same nonsense I fell for when I considered the married man as a good option to alleviate my temporary suffering. I bought into the lie that my selfish desires were more important (my flesh), I deserved it (pride), and that I could make this decision apart from God with no consequences (ego). I could be my own boss because I knew best.

Instead, I allowed my flesh to dictate and rule over me. I did not put my foot down against the enemy and choose to obey God's Word and wait upon Him and His best for my life. I did not cherish the fullness that relationship with Him brings but allowed my wretchedly lonely state to take over my focus. I did not stand firm in the knowledge that God alone is my provision. I did not understand that I was created to have dominion over my circumstances through the power of the Holy Spirit. I became a slave to sin and a slave to my flesh. I adopted a loser mentality just like Eve and then Adam did.

In my mind, I decided that God would never provide what I thought I wanted and deserved. I doubted God Himself. I did what Adam and Eve did: I declared independence from God to my own peril and detriment.

The results were immediate. God took His hand off my business and my life. Chaos ensued in every aspect of my existence, including financially. I lost most of my savings in an imprudent investment and ended up having to enter into a consumer proposal with my debtors. All this and more because I thought I knew better than my Creator what was best for me. I walked outside the palace walls and exposed my flank to the flaming arrows of my enemy. My short-term gain yielded only long-term pain. Engaging in sin always has a domino effect.

Passing the Buck

To add insult to injury, when God confronted Adam and Eve with their disobedience, neither of them owned up to their mistakes. Adam blamed Eve as well as God for Eve's failure.

The man said, "The woman whom you gave to be with me, she gave me the fruit of the tree, and I ate."
~ Genesis 3:12

Adam essentially told God, *"Look, God, You created this mess because You gave me a woman who was weak-willed. It's not my fault!"*

I've said the same thing. I told God that if only He had brought me the mate I felt was my right to have, I would not have had to go off with the married men. So really, it was His entire fault according to my sin-infected thinking.

What's that saying? *The apple doesn't fall far from the tree.* How ironic.

After God confronted Adam and heard his excuses, Eve then blamed Satan and pulled that tiresome, damsel-in-distress routine. She alleged that Satan had deceived her when, in reality, Eve had deceived herself. She knew the rules, and yet she disobeyed anyway.

Eve made a *conscious decision* to go against the order of God. She *chose* to indulge in something that she thought would improve her lot in life even though it meant a walk into disobedience. Again, it was the same argument or excuse I used to convince myself that being with a married man was the answer. I deceived myself. No one held a gun to my head.

And so, in one fell swoop, our original, earthly parents separated themselves and all of humanity from the protection of the Kingdom of God. They interrupted our original seamless and perfect relationship with the Heavenly Father. They disqualified themselves and us from our place as God's lawful ambassadors on earth and set us up to wander the earth in search of the Kingdom of God while being totally exposed and susceptible to the ruler of darkness.

At the same time, Satan pulled off the first recorded "palace coup" so to speak. Satan stole from Adam and Eve their lawful authority to be God's ambassadors on earth. The enemy overthrew Adam and Eve, taking their place as creation-keepers without having been legally appointed to the position by God. Finally, Satan destroyed the symbiotic relationship God had with Adam and Eve and that they had with each other. In effect, Satan became the rogue and illegal ruler of the earth, bringing sin into the world through God's beloved first creatures.

Consequences of Original Sin

God was none too pleased with Adam and Eve when He saw what they had done. He pronounced grave consequences upon the three of them, the effects of which the world and its inhabitants continue to experience to this day.

For Satan / the serpent:

- Would be cursed above all livestock and animals
- Would crawl on his belly
- Would eat dust all the days of his life
- Would experience enmity (animosity and hatred) between himself and the woman and between the woman's offspring and himself
- The woman's offspring (Jesus) would crush Satan's (the serpent's) head
- Satan would strike the offspring's heel

For Eve and woman:

- Greatly increased pain in childbearing
- Her desire would be for her husband
- Her husband would rule over her

For Adam and man:

- The ground would be cursed
- He would exert painful toil in order to provide for himself
- The ground would produce thorns and thistles for him to contend with
- Would have to eat the plants of the field

- Would sweat to produce food

For both the man and the woman:

- Would return to the ground as dust from whence they came
- Banished from the Garden of Eden
- Could never eat again from the Tree of Life
- Would experience death

With this one interaction, the pattern for mankind was set. We have allowed ourselves to be ruled by the lust of the flesh, the lust of the eye, or the pride of life – what we want and desire – rather than obey God, just like Adam and Eve did in the garden. When trials and temptations come – the storms of life – we can self-obsess, turning our attention inward to our distress and hurt instead of trusting God and His provision. When we take our eyes off God, we acquire a worldly mindset that works against God's intention. We doubt how God made us (in His image), and we doubt whom we are (beloved sons and daughters of the Most High King and God's ambassadors on earth). Then, we have the tendency to blame others, even God, when the proverbial dirt hits the fan. Adam and Eve set in motion the struggle of all humanity through their independence from God.

Despite the fact that on the cross Jesus defeated Satan (who to this day remains a defeated foe), Satan continuously searches the earth looking for people to devour[14]. Satan is seeking to destroy those who lack the knowledge of God, those who do not understand to whom they belong, and those who do not know God's Word and can stand firm in His promises.

Fortunately, God developed a plan to address this situation, to which we will now turn our attention.

---

[14] See 1 Peter 5:8

9

KING, INTERRUPTED

It happened one night when I was reading the Word. The Holy Spirit led me to read Psalm 51. I was as drawn to this Psalm as I was inextricably drawn to read Song of Solomon that incredible night in the mountains.

I began with the preamble, which notes that King David wrote the Psalm after the prophet Nathan confronted him. I knew something about David but not the whole story. It was time to really understand the entire sweep of King David's journey.

In 1 Samuel 15, we read that God told Samuel how He had rejected Saul as king due to Saul's disobedience to God. In fact, God *"regretted that he had made Saul king over Israel."*[15] Then, God told Samuel that he

---

[15] I Samuel 15:35

would find Saul's successor among the sons from the house of Jesse[16], and that he was to go there to anoint him. In obedience, Samuel immediately left for Jesse's house in Bethlehem.

Once at Jesse's house, Samuel first laid eyes upon Eliab, one of David's brothers. He thought to himself that this man must be the one God had sent him to anoint. Samuel likely did what we all tend to do – he judged Eliab based on how attractive he was. The Lord, however, told Samuel otherwise.

But the Lord said to Samuel, "Do not look on his appearance or on the height of his stature, because I have rejected him. For the Lord sees not as man sees: man looks on the outward appearance, but the Lord looks on the heart."
~ 1 Samuel 16:7

After seven of David's brothers were presented to Samuel with no success, Jesse mentioned his youngest son David. Man's wisdom would have thought this choice rather odd. What would a lowly, teenaged,

---

[16] I Samuel 16:1

shepherd boy know about being a king and leading the nation of Israel? Refusing to leave until his task was completed, Samuel sent for the young shepherd boy.

David was then presented to Samuel:

...And the Lord said, "Arise, anoint him, for this is he." Then Samuel took the horn of oil and anointed him in the midst of his brothers. And the Spirit of the Lord rushed upon David from that day forward....
~ 1 Samuel 16:12-13

God deposited into David a purpose as monumental as they come. At the same time, He must have known that David would later slip and fall, bringing sorrow to God, to himself, and to those around him. Yet, He still chose David as a man among men who could accomplish this kingly anointing.

God looks at our hearts and judges us based on our faithfulness to Him rather than discounting us at the outset because of our propensity to sin and experience failure. In fact, the only individuals available for God to carry out His great and wondrous purposes on this earth were and are sinful and fallen men and women. Rest here for a minute, and let this truth sink in. *There is hope for you and me in this reality.*

Before David faced Goliath with only a slingshot and five stones, he demonstrated his great faithfulness to God in a conversation with Saul. Saul doubted whether David would succeed against Goliath, a giant among warriors and who had been a fighting man since his youth. In his skepticism, Saul reminded David that he was only a boy. David responded with bravado familiar to daring, young men. With confidence, he recounted what God had done for him in the past. David boldly declared that God would ensure his success in his duel with the giant.

And David said, "The Lord who delivered me from the paw of the lion and from the paw of the bear will deliver me from the hand of this Philistine."
~ 1 Samuel 17:37a

Recognizing David's anointing, Saul told him, *"Go, and the Lord be with you!"* (1 Samuel 17:37b)

Goliath saw the young David coming towards him with his simple and meager weapons. I can only imagine his snort of arrogance and disdain at this young upstart who dared to face him, a giant and a mighty warrior.

And the Philistine said to David, "Am I a dog, that you come to me with sticks?" And the Philistine cursed David by his gods. The Philistine said to David, "Come to me, and I will give your flesh to the birds of the air and to the beasts of the field."
~ 1 Samuel 17:43-44

Full of assurance that the Lord would give him victory, David took his stand, boldly declaring:

..."You come to me with a sword and with a spear and with a javelin, but I come to you in the name of the Lord of Hosts, the God of the armies of Israel, whom you have defied. This day the Lord will deliver you into my hand, and I will strike you down and cut off your

head. And I will give the dead bodies of the host of the Philistines this day to the birds of the air and to the wild beasts of the earth, that all the earth may know that there is a God in Israel, and that all this assembly may know that the Lord saves not with sword and spear. For the battle is the Lord's, and he will give you into our hand."
~ 1 Samuel 17:45-47

God had deposited a great spirit of courage into David as a young shepherd boy. David's faithful service to God during times of testing (slaying the lion and the bear) prepared him for the greater challenge of facing Goliath. His heart was right before the Lord, and the evidence of that was demonstrated on the battlefield.

As the story goes, David then entered into Saul's court, loyally served him, and went into battle several times upon Saul's command. Eventually, however, Saul's jealous spirit and hatred of David drove the young man to flee into the wilderness. Saul was intent on murdering David, but God protected him time and time again. For about 20 years, David hid from Saul in the wilderness where he gathered an army from the outcasts of Israel. Several times, David was in a position to kill Saul but, as a man of integrity, he refused to touch the Lord's anointed.

David, whom the Bible records as a man after God's own heart, earned this reputation. He was devoted to doing things God's way, even in the face of doubts expressed by his men. David inquired of the Lord, repeatedly asking God when he should make a move, where he should go, and how he should go about what God wanted him to do. In all that he did, David gave God the glory for his many victories. Eventually, David was crowned King at Hebron (about 1000 BC) and established Jerusalem as the capital as we read in 2 Samuel, chapters 1-5.

In 2 Samuel 7, God's great intentions for David, as revealed to Nathan the prophet, are recorded.

"Go and tell my servant David, 'Thus says the Lord: Would you build me a house to dwell in? I have not lived in a house since the day I brought up the people of Israel from Egypt to

this day, but I have been moving about in a tent for my dwelling.

In all places where I have moved with all the people of Israel, did I speak a word with any of the judges of Israel, whom I commanded to shepherd My people Israel, saying, "Why have you not built me a house of cedar?"'

Now, therefore, thus you shall say to my servant David, 'Thus says the Lord of hosts, I took you from the pasture, from following the sheep, that you should be prince over my people Israel.

And I have been with you wherever you went and have cut off all your enemies before you. And I will make for you a great name, like the name of the great ones of the earth.

And I will appoint a place for my people Israel and will plant them, so that they may dwell in their own place and be disturbed no more. And violent men shall afflict them no more, as formerly, from the time that I appointed judges over my people Israel. And I will give you rest from all your enemies. Moreover, the Lord declares to you that the Lord will make you a house.

When your days are fulfilled and you lie down with your fathers, I will raise up your offspring after you, who shall come from your body, and I will establish his kingdom.

He shall build a house for my name, and I will establish the throne of his kingdom forever.

I will be to him a father, and he shall be to me a son. When he commits iniquity, I will discipline him with the rod of men, with the stripes of the sons of men, but my steadfast love will not depart from him, as I took it from Saul, whom I put away from before you.

And your house and your kingdom shall be made sure forever before me. Your throne shall be established forever.'"

In accordance with all these words, and in accordance with all this vision, Nathan spoke to David.

~ 2 Samuel 7:5-17

God established David as He promised. David ruled from the fortress in Jerusalem. As part of his God-ordained mission, he brought the Ark of the Covenant there as its permanent resting place.

And then it happened. For a split second, David diverted his eyes and heart away from God. He gave in to his own selfish and sinful desires.

One day, when other kings and his own men were at war, David walked around on the rooftop of his palace. From his vantage point, he spied the beautiful Bathsheba next door taking a bath. Bathsheba was married to Uriah the Hittite who was also away at war fighting on behalf of David.

Abusing his royal authority, David ordered his messengers to bring Bathsheba to his chambers. He then committed adultery with her.[17] Not caring that she was a married woman, he seduced her, giving in to his selfish desires for his own pleasure.

When David learned that Bathsheba was pregnant with his child, he attempted to hide his wrongdoing by ordering her husband in from the front lines. The plan was for Uriah to come home to be with his wife so that it

---

[17] See 2 Samuel 11

could reasonably be concluded by everyone that Bathsheba's child was her husband's offspring.

Uriah, however, possessed more integrity than David anticipated. Uriah refused to spend time with his wife in the comfort of his home while his fellow men were suffering on the battlefield. He slept at the entrance to his home instead of with his wife.

David then concocted an elaborate scheme to cover up his sin given that Uriah would not sleep with his wife. He arranged for Uriah to be killed at battle, thereby making it possible for David to avoid being accused of fathering Bathsheba's child. David's intention behind his order – ensuring that Uriah was killed – came to its painful conclusion.

Engulfed in selfishness, pride, and sin, David ended up inflicting pain and tragedy upon himself, Uriah, and Bathsheba in exchange for the temporary pleasures of self-indulgence. Worse yet, he had displeased God.

When the wife of Uriah heard that Uriah her husband was dead, she lamented over her husband. And when the mourning was over, David sent and brought her to his house, and she became his wife and bore him a son. But the thing that David had done displeased the Lord.
~ 2 Samuel 11:26-27

The Bible tells us plainly that the Lord sees whatever a man does, whether it is in secret or in broad daylight. In this case, David's actions, including his cover-up plan, were a stench to God.

Once again, God mobilized His prophet Nathan to speak His words. Nathan went to the palace to confront David with his sin. Using a parable, he described to David his own actions:

And the Lord sent Nathan to David. He came to him and said to him, "There were two men in a certain city, the one rich and the other poor. The rich man had very many flocks and herds, but the poor man had nothing but one little ewe lamb, which he had bought. And he brought it up, and it grew up with him and with his children. It used to eat of his morsel and drink from his cup and lie in his arms, and it was like a daughter to him. Now there came a traveler to the rich man, and he was unwilling to take one of his own flock or herd to prepare for the guest who had come to him, but he took the poor man's lamb and prepared it for the man who had come to him."

Then David's anger was greatly kindled against the man, and he said to Nathan, "As the Lord lives, the man who has done this deserves to die, and he shall restore the lamb fourfold, because he did this thing, and because he had no pity."

Nathan said to David, "You are the man! Thus says the Lord, the God of Israel, 'I anointed you king over Israel, and I delivered you out of the hand of Saul. And I gave you your master's house and your master's wives into your arms and gave you the house of Israel and of Judah. And if this were too little, I would add to you as much more. Why have you despised the word of the Lord, to do what is evil in His sight? You have struck down Uriah the Hittite with the sword and have taken his wife to be your wife and have killed him with the sword of the Ammonites. Now therefore the sword shall never depart from your house, because you have despised Me and have taken the wife of Uriah the Hittite to be your wife.' Thus says the Lord, 'Behold, I will raise up evil against you out of your own house. And I will take your wives before your eyes and give them to your neighbor, and he shall lie with your wives in the sight of this sun. For you did it secretly, but I will do this thing before all Israel and before the sun.'"

David said to Nathan, "I have sinned against the Lord."

And Nathan said to David, "The Lord also has put away your sin; you shall not die. Nevertheless, because by this deed you have utterly scorned the Lord, the child who is born to you shall die."
~ 2 Samuel 12:1-14

Despite David's subsequent petition before God with prayer and fasting, Bathsheba's baby died after seven days of illness. As Scripture says, David had shown an utter contempt for the Lord through his giving in to sin...and the consequences proved grave and painful.

Upon David's confession, God took David's sin away. However, his sin had far-reaching consequences. There is always a price to be paid for indulging in sin habits of the flesh.

From the beginning to the end, God knows all. He had selected David as a teenager to be king over all Israel. This was an edict that God would not revoke, even in the face of David's future sin that God must have surely foreseen.

Anointed by God, David became the most famous king of Israel and produced more children, including the great King Solomon. Furthermore, some twenty-seven generations later, Jesus Christ entered the world through the House of David, a name that endures to this day.

When God was dealing with my sin habits with the married men, He took the sin away as He promises to do for anyone who confesses their sin and repents. As 1 John

1:9 states, *"If we confess our sins, He is faithful and just to forgive us our sins and to cleanse us from all unrighteousness."* However, just like with David, I was also brought to the point where I was faced with my iniquities and the full ramifications of what I had done.

I, too, had to admit to myself and to God that I had treated the Lord with utter contempt. Although no one was murdered, I had assaulted God and had inflicted pain and distress upon myself, as well as upon the second married man along with his wife who was informed of the situation. And God did not stop there. He took His hand off my life and business, both of which started unraveling like a scarf off the knitting needles. My finances went totally awry, and the situation with one of my children grew considerably worse. I was overwhelmed with worry much of the time and was incapable of fixing the shambles that had become my life.

In my sin, I was like David – blinded to all reason and sensibility and a slave to my sin habit. The depth of my assault against God did not even register given that I had completely turned away from focusing on Him in order to satisfy my desires of the flesh. There had to be a pivotal point that would open my eyes to see where I was going astray. I ended up having to come to the end of myself and see my relationship with Alex dissolve before God could get my attention.

It was not until Nathan rebuked David that David's eyes were supernaturally opened. Then, he finally understood the depth of his immorality and experienced heartfelt remorse and conviction over his actions. Sometimes it takes someone else confronting us with our sin before we can fully comprehend our transgressions against God.

Psalm 51 is David's confessional written after Nathan had confronted him. As a psalm of appeal before God, it beautifully expresses David's understanding and acknowledgement of his own utter brokenness and wretchedness before the Lord. I experienced the same depth of emotion after the Holy Spirit opened my eyes to my lifelong, relational recklessness.

Notice that Psalm 51 is not a paltry "I'm sorry, God. I'll try harder next time." Instead, Psalm 51 is a desolate, heart-wrenching plea for mercy. It is a detailed account of David's sin. It is the ultimate picture of accountability as it is David's understanding that he needed to, with complete honesty, name and own up to his sin before God, verbally acknowledging the evil that he had engaged in before the Lord. Psalm 51 also shows David's comprehension that God is to be feared, not in a scared or fearful way, but rather as One who is all-knowing and all-powerful.

I love Psalm 51 because it reminds me of that pivotal moment when God had me face my own iniquities as a believer. In His love and mercy, He rendered judgment (conviction) and grace (forgiveness) all at once. Psalm 51 brings to mind the absolute necessity and beauty of a broken (humbled) and contrite (remorseful) heart.

To enter back into God's Presence, and in order to live once again under the mantle of His peace that passes all understanding, we must come to a place of willing adherence to

His laws and the guidance of the Holy Spirit. This restoration is sweeter than any other experience on this earth.

So how do we get to this glorious place of willing obedience to God and of restoration in His Presence? We will address this most important question next.

10

THE KEYS TO RESTORATION

"The pattern of the prodigal is: rebellion, ruin, repentance, reconciliation, restoration."

Edwin Louis Cole

Before we consider how to unlock the door to restoration, a prayerful read of Psalm 51 seems appropriate.

1 Have mercy on me, O God, according to your steadfast love; according to your abundant mercy blot out my transgressions.
2 Wash me thoroughly from my iniquity, and cleanse me from my sin!
3 For I know my transgressions, and my sin is ever before me.
4 Against you, you only, have I sinned and done what is evil in your sight, so that you may be

justified in your words and blameless in your judgment.
5 Behold, I was brought forth in iniquity, and in sin did my mother conceive me.
6 Behold, you delight in truth in the inward being, and you teach me wisdom in the secret heart.
7 Purge me with hyssop, and I shall be clean; wash me, and I shall be whiter than snow.
8 Let me hear joy and gladness; let the bones that you have broken rejoice.
9 Hide your face from my sins, and blot out all my iniquities.
10 Create in me a clean heart, O God, and renew a right spirit within me.
11 Cast me not away from your presence, and take not your Holy Spirit from me.
12 Restore to me the joy of your salvation and uphold me with a willing spirit.
13 Then I will teach transgressors your ways, and sinners will return to you.
14 Deliver me from bloodguiltiness, O God, O God of my salvation, and my tongue will sing aloud of your righteousness.
15 O Lord, open my lips, and my mouth will declare your praise.

16 For you will not delight in sacrifice, or I would give it; you will not be pleased with a burnt offering.
17 The sacrifices of God are a broken spirit; a broken and contrite heart, O God, you will not despise.
18 Do good to Zion in your good pleasure; build up the walls of Jerusalem;
19 then will you delight in right sacrifices, in burnt offerings and whole burnt offerings; then bulls will be offered on your alter.

Psalm 51 opens with David appealing to God in what I imagine was like a death row plea for clemency before a panel of Supreme Court judges: *"Have mercy on me, O God, according to your steadfast love; according to your abundant mercy blot out my transgressions."* In this one small sentence, David realized three important things we all must understand when we sin.

1. *When we sin, we sin against God.* Notice that David did not mention Bathsheba or Uriah anywhere in this Psalm. Although he may have apologized to those he hurt and asked for forgiveness, they were not his primary focus. Yes, they were victimized by

David's sin, but David knew that his real problem was that he had sinned against God. I, too, must realize that my primary problem when I sin is that it is an offence against God, and it separates me from Him.

2. *God is unfailing Love and Compassion, and David was quick to remind God of that.* David appealed to God like a wise lawyer would appeal to the Court, reminding it of its authority or discretion to grant the desired verdict. I must humble myself and ask God for clemency knowing that only He is capable of cleansing me from all unrighteousness. I cannot do that for myself.

3. *We must repent and seek God's forgiveness for our sins or transgressions.* We have to call a spade a spade and a sin a sin. We can't avert our eyes from our own sin if we are serious about walking in the centre of God's will for our lives.

Another psalm of David, Psalm 32, also speaks directly to the imperative of confessing our sins and seeking repentance from God.

1 Blessed is the one whose transgression is forgiven, whose sin is covered.

2 Blessed is the man against whom the Lord counts no iniquity, and in whose spirit there is no deceit.

3 For when I kept silent, my bones wasted away through my groaning all day long.

4 For day and night your hand was heavy upon me; my strength was dried up as by the heat of summer.   Selah

5 I acknowledged my sin to you, and I did not cover my iniquity; I said, "I will confess my transgressions to the Lord," and you forgave the iniquity of my sin.   Selah

6 Therefore let everyone who is godly offer prayer to you at a time when you may be found; surely in the rush of great waters, they shall not reach him.

7 You are a hiding place for me; you preserve me from trouble; you surround me with shouts of deliverance.   Selah

8 I will instruct you and teach you in the way you should go; I will counsel you with My eye upon you.

9 Be not like a horse or a mule, without understanding, which must be curbed with bit and bridle, or it will not stay near you.

10 Many are the sorrows of the wicked, but steadfast love surrounds the one who trusts in the Lord.

11 Be glad in the Lord, and rejoice, O righteous, and shout for joy, all you upright of heart!

David realized that unconfessed sin resulted in grave consequences. His bones would waste away, as in his health would be affected. He would spend his life groaning and suffering under heaviness and futility where his mental and physical state would be drastically affected with no direction, spiritual or otherwise. The price we pay for unconfessed sin is always our own discomfort.

Our lives do not work properly when we harbour sin in our hearts. Everything is a struggle, a burden, and a worry. We cannot fulfill the purpose God has designed us to fulfill when we refuse to repent of our sins. When we stand in our own will and go our own way, God is not free to move on our behalf, and our lives become as barren as they were before we were saved.

God as a *"Hiding Place"*

In Psalm 32:7, David refers to God as his *"hiding place"* and a place of protection and surrounding love.

Do you find that when you walk uprightly and in obedience to God's Word that you are surrounded with His peace that passes all understanding, even if a storm is raging all around you? Equally, have you ever noticed how out of sorts you feel when you are walking in sin and how off-centre and easily upset you become? I certainly have.

When I was walking in sin with married men, nothing in my life was flowing smoothly. My business nearly folded. My one child ran amuck. I was plagued with many worries rather than operating with a trust in God. Even though I felt that I deserved the love a man could give me, I did not connect my sinful pursuit of that love to my life falling apart all around me.

When I elevated my sin habit above all else, making it the treasure of my heart, I forsook the God who saved me from hell. I was not in the Word, and my prayer-life was non-existent. As a result, my life was an uncomfortable grind against a sharp stone. I was no better than the stubborn mule that would not stay close to its master as David refers to in Psalm 32:9.

Let us now consider the essential teachings found in Psalm 51. They serve as keys to unlocking the door to restoration. We begin with Psalm 51:4.

Key #1: *Against you, you only, have I sinned and done what is evil in your sight.*

In that mountain cabin, this was exactly what Jesus showed me: that I had re-nailed Jesus to the cross with my sin. I had rejected the life-giving teachings that God had placed in my heart and had grieved the Holy Spirit. That jagged realization broke my heart.

I looked again upon the pitiable sight of Jesus on the cross at Calvary, a sight that God described as being marred beyond human recognition[18], and I was convicted. The

---

[18] Isaiah 52:14

problem was not that I had caused a few human beings some unnecessary pain. The problem was that I had broken my covenant – my spiritual bond and connection – with my dear Lord and Savior who endured the unspeakable in order that I might be united in Spirit with Him, the Living God, the Creator and Lover of my soul.

Yes, indeed. Sin is an assault against God.

Let's get real for a moment. Sinful activity is usually pleasurable. Pleasure is seductive, and we love it. Sin is also attractive and addictive. Using this against us, Satan tempts us with the lie that no one will find out about it if we go ahead and act out in sin. We probably all recognize the saying, *"What happens in Vegas, stays in Vegas."* Pushing this mentality, Satan tricks us into believing that we can keep our sin hidden or contained, not having it affect our "real" lives. Worse yet, he manipulates our mind into rationalizing sin as being "okay" and that we will never have to pay for our indulgence.

This is the lie of all lies.

Sin is never confined to the incident in question. Instead, it seeps out through the cracks, infecting everything and everyone in its path. In a brief moment, sin can ruin relationships and destroy families. Sin can destroy businesses and even topple governments. It can ruin reputations and bring on unending grief and despair. Indulging in sin is never without a cost.

Is whatever momentary pleasure sin brings to us really worth the ruin it brings into our lives? This was a question that had I never asked myself, but certainly wished I had.

We turn next to Psalm 51:10a.

Key #2: *Create in me a clean heart, O God.*

Satan wants us to believe that we are able to self-regulate, in particular our own desires, and that we don't need God to direct our paths and our ways. One of his goals is to persuade us to ignore God and make our own plans. This was the same ploy he used against Adam and Eve in the Garden, and it continues to be one of his main methods of attack: *Follow your heart because it knows best what you need and desire. If it "feels" good, then it is right for you.*

This idea of *following our own heart*, including letting feelings rule our heart and subsequent decisions, is what the world is peddling today, at least in North America. We hear it everywhere we go: *Have it your way...look within where the answers are...pursue your heart's desire...*and on and on and on.

I would love nothing more than to be able to follow my own heart without having to constantly seek and trust God for my every move. Unfortunately, the reality is that my heart has consistently led me into dark places, as it most assuredly did with those married men. The heart, left to its own devices, is untrustworthy.

The enemy would like nothing better than to have us doubt God and the relevance and importance of His commands and precepts for our lives. He wants us to think that God doesn't know what He is doing. He is out to convince us that He doesn't "know" us and, therefore, does not understand our needs. Ultimately, Satan is out to persuade us to believe that God cannot be trusted when it comes to the matters of our own heart, mind, body, and soul.

Satan is a liar!

Does the potter not know how to form the clay? Does the architect not know how the house he or she designed needs to be built and maintained? In the same way, can we not conclude that the One who conceived us in His own mind and heart before we came into being and then formed us in all our uniqueness and intricacies knows *exactly* what we need at all times, *including* what we need to avoid in order to live free from bondage and defeat? Can He not be trusted to guide us away from sin and into righteousness, especially as He has not left us without direction and help because He has provided us with His written Word and the Helper – the Holy Spirit? As believers, we should know the answers to these questions.

By asking God to create in him a clean and pure heart, David admitted that, in his own strength and will, he was incapable of having and keeping a pure heart. Again, I experienced great relief when I read that! I had renewed hope!

I can ask God to give me what I need to help me resist temptation!

Let us take a lesson from King David, the greatest King in the history of Israel. Observe how quickly he admitted his wrongdoing when he was faced with it. Consider his realization of his own helplessness to create within himself a pure and obedient heart. Finally, notice how he petitioned and relied on God to give him a heart that was inclined toward righteousness. Let us learn from David's example and cry out, *"Create in me a clean heart, O God!"* This is my daily prayer now, and I pray that this would become yours as well.

We next look at Psalm 51:10b.

Key #3: *Renew a right spirit within me.*

There is such hope in these few words: renew a right spirit within me. Even our faith is a gift from God and is not possible without the supernatural work of the Holy Spirit. Have you ever considered that? I must say that I had not. I figured that I needed to muster my own will power and discipline to keep my spirit right – or steadfast – and trained and focused upon God. What a relief to know that even the great King David had to ask God to give him a steadfast spirit! I, too, did not have to walk out my faith in my own strength.

I now know, beyond all doubt, that I cannot be steadfast or right within my spirit without the work of the Holy Spirit. I have discovered and experienced that God is faithful and kind to give me what I need to stay obedient to Him when I ask Him. He is always there, ready to help me on my journey.

Then, there is that wonderful word: *renew.* This word offers to every believer the hope of restoration after sin. It means that we can have a new start in Jesus and in the God of new beginnings. It is the most wondrous, glorious promise for every believer!

As we survey the entirety of King David's life, we see that his affair with Bathsheba occurred in the middle of his journey with God. We are shown that David's sinful interlude did not stop him from completing his assignment from God. Why? Because David realized his grievous sin against God and earnestly repented, he was able to continue on the path of fulfilling God's plan for his life.

God *renewed* David's steadfast spirit.

Sin will take us out of the game and off of our Divinely appointed path *if we let it.* If we refuse to repent of our sin habits and submit to the direction of God and His transforming power, we get off track, missing out on the fullness of God's blessings in our lives.

You see, when we allow our sinful nature to take flight and rule our life, Satan swoops in to whisper yet another, dirty lie into our ears. He plants within our minds that when we sin as a believer, we are washed up forever and, therefore, no good to God. The enemy works overtime to convince us that once we sin, God will not bring to conclusion the plans that He has for us. He aims to steal our hope and our future.

Yet, we see from David's life that it is not our sin per se that disqualifies us from God's Kingdom purposes being realized in our lives. What disqualifies us from our calling, including unhindered fellowship with God and His anointing upon our lives, is our unwillingness to confess our sins, repent, and ask God to give us, not only a pure and clean heart, but also a willing spirit to live a life sold out for Him.

Don't miss this point, for it is pivotal to our lives as believers.

It is God and God alone who gives us a pure and clean heart *AND* the right spirit and capability to walk in purity and obedience to Him.

Our job is to remain humble in His Presence, to immediately repent of our sins as often as they occur, and to stay close to God with our eyes securely affixed upon Him and His Word.

Now, please do not think that I am advocating using these verses as "fire insurance" so that we can repeatedly and wilfully sin time and time again, never making a clean break from our transgressions. To misuse God's gracious forgiveness after we repeatedly sin and continue to do as we want is as repugnant as using abortions as a method of birth control. Knowing that God is there ready to forgive us of all our sin is not a license for selfish indulgence.

No, God's provision of forgiveness and renewal is never an excuse to sin. It is reckless of us to think that we can carry on in our sinful habits without consequences. God's desire is to cleanse us from all unrighteousness.[19]

---

[19] See 1 John 1:9

Our next step is to realize the consequences of our sin as stated in Psalm 51:11.

Key #4: *Cast me not away from your presence, and take not your Holy Spirit from me.*

David realized something that we don't often hear in many of our churches today. Sin separates us from the fellowship of God and causes God to turn away from our prayers. Sin moves us out from under His protective covering and away from His comforting peace that passes all understanding.

But your iniquities have made a separation between you and your God, and your sins have hidden his face from you so that he does not hear.
~ Isaiah 59:2

This is no joke! Our sin separates us from God's Presence and protection. I know the truth of this verse because I experienced it. I believe Scripture says it best:

For if we go on sinning deliberately after receiving the knowledge of the truth, there no longer remains a sacrifice for sins, but a fearful expectation of judgment, and a fury of fire that will consume the adversaries. Anyone who has set aside the law of Moses dies without mercy on the evidence of two or three witnesses. How much worse punishment, do you think, will be deserved by the one who has trampled underfoot the Son of God, and has profaned the blood of the covenant by which he was sanctified, and has outraged the Spirit of grace? For we know him who said, "Vengeance is mine; I will repay." And again, "The Lord will judge his people." It is a fearful thing to fall into the hands of the living God.
~ Hebrews 10:26-31

I can attest to the fact that it is definitely a dangerous thing to fall into the hands of the living God. I can also say with equal certainty that where sin is great yet brokenness and contrition are real, Grace and Mercy are greater still and overflow to cleanse the repentant heart.

This brings us to the next key found in Psalm 51:17.

Key #5: *** The sacrifices of God are a broken spirit; a broken and contrite heart, O God, you will not despise.***

After his fall with Bathsheba, David experienced a total collapse of his arrogance and wilful self-governance. By God's great Grace, David experienced a broken and contrite heart, meaning he humbled himself before the Lord with true remorse. We see in Psalm 51:7 God's assurance that He will never despise or turn away from those who are genuinely repentant. David turned away from his sin and did not return to that behaviour. This is what God impressed upon me in reading through this psalm, and it's something we all must do to be in right relationship with God.

The Holy Spirit showed me that revival follows repentance, repentance follows conviction, and conviction follows brokenness. All are a supernatural working of the Spirit of God and His great and profound Mercy and Grace in our lives.

The sacrifice that God requires is, therefore, a heart that is soft and humbled towards Him. He desires the sacrifice of a heart that is truly repentant. With this type of heart, He can bring about the restoration He has promised.

Our next step is to apprehend a beautiful truth found in Psalm 51:12.

Key #6: *Restore to me the joy of your salvation, and uphold me with a willing spirit.*

David was restored to fellowship with God after he repented. In fact, David was not only restored to right relationship with God, but God granted David the same joy that he experienced when he first experienced salvation. He did so even amidst David's subsequent struggles and battles. What hope there is in this verse!

Moreover, we understand from this passage that we cannot maintain a willing spirit to remain faithful to God on our own except by His Grace. For me, this felt like a huge weight had been lifted off my shoulders. I have grasped onto the truth that I don't have to ever rely only on myself to maintain my allegiance to God. He will grant me a willing spirit if I only ask.

If you have believed the lie that, once you sin as a believer, God will reject you forever, memorize verses 10-11 from Psalm 51. They highlight four of the six keys to restoration that I have shared here. In these verses, you will find hope and promise for how to return to the heart and Presence of God. Furthermore, remind yourself of verse 17 (Key #5) that gives us our greatest weapon against defeat: a broken and contrite heart.

God loves genuine brokenness and contrition, not because He is a sadist, but because when we stand before Him in humbleness of heart with sincere remorse for what we have done wrong, we grant Him permission to be our Daddy and Friend and Rescuer. We acknowledge that He is God, and we are not. It opens us up to receive that willing spirit (Key #6) that will help us obey and pursue God.

When we submit to God in a posture of humility and honest repentance, we are really at our most wise. Throughout the Bible, we are reminded that to honour God is to be a good steward of our life and brings about the blessings of God. It is the chief mandate for all of mankind.

When we adopt a genuine attitude of humility, we allow God to be God, and we give ourselves every opportunity to "straighten up and fly right", as the song sung by The King Cole Trio[20] says. It is with this right attitude, or right spirit, that our lives will soar into the heights of God's Will and Grace and Mercy and Peace. It allows us to be at peace even in the middle of the worst crisis. And who doesn't want peace?

Restoration after a believer sins, therefore, is simple yet impossible without God's Grace, Mercy, and the working of the Holy Spirit. Here, then, is a recipe to help us stay out of the death grip of sin:

---

[20] Song written by Nat King Cole and Irving Mills

1. ***Daily maintain a genuine attitude of brokenness and contrition.*** This means we must immediately repent of sin and our assault against God. *Decide* to never indulge in that sin again. *Commit* yourself to *act* in accordance with that decision. Stay away from places, people, situations, media, thoughts, etc., that you know will lead you into that sin. Most importantly, you *DECIDE, COMMIT, and ACT* under the power of the Holy Spirit for you cannot do this in your own strength.

2. ***Ask God to give you a clean and pure heart along with a willing and steadfast spirit.*** The condition of your heart and your willingness to operate under a right spirit will facilitate you being able to joyfully obey His commands and precepts for your life. Again, understand that it is only by the power of the Holy Spirit that you can even want to stay away from sin. So, ask for these things and *you shall receive!*

3. ***Understand that the gravest result of sin is broken fellowship with God.*** Our sin removes us from God's Presence and protection, which is a dangerous place to be.

Ask God to keep your heart pure and desirous of being in the centre of His will at all times.

4. ***Ask God to restore you after you have sinned, and He will!*** Do not listen to the lies of Satan that after you sin as a believer, you are washed up and rejected by God. This is rubbish! David's life is a testimony of the fact that IF we remain humble and are willing to REPENT and seek God for restoration to righteousness, He will be quick to forgive us and only too happy to restore us to the path and purposes He has designed for us.

Let's Pray:

Heavenly Father, we come to You now with a broken and contrite heart. We understand that, when we sin, we sin against You and You only. We know that, on our own, we are incapable of having a faithful and steadfast heart. Our selfish and independent hearts are naturally inclined away from You, and yet, You are our very breath and life. Without Your lifeblood coursing through our veins, our lives are meaningless and small. Thank you, dear Father, that through the power of the Holy

Spirit, our hearts can once again be inclined towards You, our spirits can be made faithful and steadfast, and we can be renewed and restored to fellowship with You. Then, we can enjoy Your Presence fully and hear from You all that You would have us know. Thank you, Jesus, for what You endured on the cross for us. Help us this day to not trample You underfoot or treat as insignificant and unholy the Blood of the covenant that sanctified us. Thank you, Holy Spirit, for helping us to not insult the Spirit of Grace. In Jesus' Name. Amen.

11

PUTTING IT ALL TOGETHER

It is my hope that my story has encouraged you to look within to see where you might be struggling with a cycle of indulging in sin habits, including relational recklessness. Maybe you are frustrated and disappointed in your own walk as a believer. Perhaps you've paused long enough to consider your own history and life struggles and are seeing patterns or difficulties that you have been unable or unwilling to release. Hopefully, the penny has dropped, and you are now understanding yourself in a much more profound way.

Now is the time to genuinely repent of old habits and deeply entrenched sins that cannot be simply wished away. It's time to put a stake in the ground and say "No!" to relational recklessness or whatever sin has you in its death grip. Surrender to the Lord your bad habits, deep hurts, habitual sins, and whatever else you are holding onto that is getting in the way of right relationship with Him. It is *time* to do this once and for all so that you can walk in true victory knowing that you are free from the crushing burden of sin.

Once you do this, you are free to be exactly who God made you to be. You are now free to fully express your God-given gifts, talents, and abilities for the benefit of the whole world and for the glory of God. You are free to be a noble soldier in God's army to help usher in the Kingdom of God here on earth. You are now free to walk in the ease of His will with the Holy Spirit to help guide you. You are FREE!

So, let's look at what we can do in tandem with Jesus to walk in victory, moving forward successfully so that we do not relapse into sin habits of the past:

Step One – Looking Back

Ask God to show you what you need to see that will illuminate how you developed the bad habits, knee-jerk reactions, and self-serving tendencies of the past. It is necessary to analyze the past with the purpose of understanding how you got there in the first place. God has the wisdom and insight you need to highlight exactly how Satan has taken advantage of and manipulated you.

Ask Jesus to reveal to you your "family of origin" issues that have set you up to stumble and fall prey to Satan's temptations. Go back to Chapters 2 and 4 and review your answers to the reflection questions. These will help give you a clearer picture of what events or circumstances may have shaped you and why. You will understand your "why behind the why" which is one of the best places to start on your pathway to permanent change.

But remember, our objective is not to settle into our "way back then" and live in the past. Instead, we *briefly visit* the past in order to understand our beginnings – those circumstances out of which we developed habits and thought patterns that are now holding us back from freedom and victory in Christ. So, go ahead and review your answers for the purpose of understanding your weaknesses so that you can better protect yourself by making the necessary adjustments that will guard against falling into sin in the future.

Step Two – Expose and Renounce Your Sin

Turn back to Chapter 4 and 5 and review your answers to the reflection questions again. This is where the rubber hits the road. Brutal honesty was needed then, and it is needed now.

What sin are you committing? What are your justifications for committing that sin? Get real and honest here. God sees it all anyway. There's no hiding from Him, so you might as well admit it to yourself. Besides, once you have admitted it to yourself, and perhaps to an accountability partner, the worst is over.

Sin that is hidden is a much greater and potent cancer than a sin that is exposed and acknowledged for what it is. Satan loves to keep us in shame about our sin because shame keeps us quiet about our desperation. Don't be quiet about your sin! Tell someone trustworthy about it and enlist his or her support in your journey to healing!

Remember, Satan does not want us to admit our sins to each other because he doesn't want us to seek God's help to get out of the situation. Instead, his goal is that we stay in bondage and defeat and shame. Satan loves to keep things hidden and in the dark.

Take yourself out of the dark room and ruin the photos by exposing sin to the light of Jesus! This is a vital step. It sets you securely on the path that leads away from defeat and toward victory in Jesus under the power of His strength.

It is critical to remember that none of this work can take place in isolation from Jesus and without His strength. We can't even be honest with ourselves without the Holy Spirit working within us. So don't try to do this without the power of the Holy Spirit. Get an accountability buddy if you need to, making sure the person loves you enough to pray with you and hold you accountable.

Here is a great Scripture from Paul that reminds us to be vigilant about what we pay attention to and to what we accept as truth:

> *But I am afraid that as the serpent deceived Eve by his cunning, your thoughts will be led astray from a sincere and pure devotion to Christ. For if someone comes and proclaims another Jesus than the one we proclaimed, or if you receive a different spirit from the one you received, or if you accept a different gospel from the one you accepted, you put up with it readily enough.*
> ~ 2 Corinthians 11:3-4

Paul was actually writing about false prophets or teachers in this passage. There will always be counterfeits out there. We need the Holy Spirit to help us discern God's Gospel and Truth so that we aren't led astray. You cannot renounce sin if you can't identify it, including those sins that *seem* like they are okay or can be rationalized away and justified by faulty standards like I did with mine. We must be on guard to keep the faith according to God's Word. Godly accountability partners can help us with this as well.

Step Three – Repent like David

Go back to Chapter 10 and review the steps that David took when he was faced with his own sin. Once you have figured out what sin habit you need to get rid of, you need to go beyond a blanket "God, please forgive me of my sin." We have to call a spade a spade. We need to know exactly what we are repenting for. We ought to humble ourselves to the point of identifying our sin by its name and details.

Go ahead and reread Chapter 9 in addition to memorizing the key verses highlighted out of Psalm 51. Pray these Scriptures back to God in a humble plea of repentance and a request for help.

Step Four – Recommit Yourself to God

We all have to do this every now and then. Do not feel badly if you have to do this as a result of falling into sin. The important thing is that every day we make a choice – a commitment – to follow God's Word and plan for our lives. When we get off track, it is equally important to recommit our lives to God and His ways.

We are imperfect human beings hardwired to sin because of Adam and Eve's fall in the Garden. We can't even keep our hearts steadfast and focused on God without the assistance and power of the Holy Spirit! We cannot expect to walk in victory without asking God to give us a steadfast heart and willing spirit to be faithful to Him, just like David did.

And whatever we do, we simply cannot listen to the lies of Satan. We are *not* washed up and worthless once we have fallen into sin as a believer. No, we are still in need of our Savior, who is willing and able to help us get back on track when we turn our hearts to Him.

Remember the mighty King David. He completed his Divinely appointed life mission BECAUSE he repented and asked for God's help after he had sinned. Let David's example be our model!

Step Five – Engage in the Spiritual Disciplines

There is no way around this. We have to be about the Father's business each and every day. This means we ought to daily study the Word, invite the Holy Spirit to move in our hearts, and be in unity with other believers. We also need to develop and nurture our prayer life, which fosters our love relationship with God.

If you don't do this already, now is a perfect time to develop what I call the "Four Christian Disciplines". We will look at each one now.

1. <u>Study God's Word Daily</u>

    The Bible speaks of how we are to study God's Word – meditating on it, digesting it, and living it, as it is written. If we want all of God's Presence, all of His guidance and power, and all of His knowledge and wisdom to help us avoid defeat, we have to press in and be disciplined about studying the Word on a daily basis.

If you have never committed to a daily devotional and prayer time with God before, you are in for a real treat. You don't have to feel pressured to read the Bible in one year. Just dig into even one chapter per day, making notes in a journal on what the passage means to you.

Another profitable exercise is to write out a prayer of thanksgiving, praying God's Word back to Him. This is exceptionally powerful and will really help you digest God's Word. The time you spend with Him will be sweeter than anything else you have experienced in your life. I promise! So start today, and begin to reap the benefits that await you.

Here are a few Scriptures that reveal the benefits of being in God's Word daily:

For it is no empty word for you, but your very life, and by this word you shall live long in the land that you are going over the Jordan to possess." (Deuteronomy 32:47)

It is the Spirit who gives life; the flesh is no help at all. The words that I have spoken to you are spirit and life. (John 6:63)

I have stored up your word in my heart, that I might not sin against you. (Psalm 119:11)

All Scripture is breathed out by God and profitable for teaching, for reproof, for correction, and for training in righteousness. (2 Timothy 3:16)

Until I come, devote yourself to the public reading of Scripture, to exhortation, to teaching. (1 Timothy 4:13)

2. <u>Pray Daily</u>

   We all know that if we cherish a friendship or marriage, we want to daily feed it with love and care, along with developing excellent, two-way, respectful communication. It is the same with our relationship with God. We need to listen to God and to what He is speaking to us about. Prayer is one of the main ways that we communicate with God. He loves to hear our prayers and to hear us ask for His wisdom, guidance, and help.

3. <u>Be Holy-Spirit Filled</u>

   As believers, we have the Holy Spirit residing inside of us. He is not somewhere else or far away. He is right inside of us – ready, willing, and able to spring into action when called upon. In fact, there is no other power as great as that of the Holy Spirit, the same Spirit that caused Jesus to rise up from the dead! So, if the Holy Spirit can raise Jesus from the grave, don't you think He can help you in your hour of distress and harassment by the enemy? Of course He can! And He will if we ask with humility and sincerity.

Ephesians 5:18 tells us to be filled with the Spirit. God said that because He knows that we cannot stay free from the bondage of sin without Him. The Holy Spirit helps us in our weakness[21].

It takes God's power – the enabling of the Holy Spirit – and not our own will power to be free of sin.

4. <u>Fellowship with Other Believers</u>

There is strength in numbers, which explains why Satan constantly whispers in our ears that we don't need to go to church, attend Bible study, or fellowship with our fellow believers. Whenever you think those thoughts, know that Satan is attacking you. He will do whatever he can to isolate you and prevent you from being in an atmosphere of faith.

---

[21] See Romans 8:26

Hebrews states it clearly:

And let us consider how to stir up one another to love and good works, not neglecting to meet together, as is the habit of some, but encouraging one another, and all the more as you see the Day drawing near. (Hebrews 10:24-25)

Here are some other, wonderful Scriptures that remind us why we should congregate and pray with other believers:

And though a man might prevail against one who is alone, two will withstand him – a threefold cord is not quickly broken. (Ecclesiastes 4:12)

Therefore, confess your sins to one another and pray for one another, that you may be healed. The prayer of a righteous person has great power as it is working. (James 5:16)

Step Six – Take Dead Aim

Professional golfers talk about taking "dead aim" at the target on the golf course. The target is either a particular spot on the fairway or it's on the putting green. Regardless, the best golfers always train their minds on the target, visualizing the ball's flight – how the ball will leave the clubface, how it will rise into the air, where it will bounce, and where it will come to rest – all before they take a swing. In their minds, they take "dead aim" toward the target, having already seen the shot completed in their imagination before they step up to hit the ball.

This is what we need to do to be righteous and holy in God's sight. We need to focus our attention on God and be intentional about all our thoughts, speech, and actions. By visualizing ourselves as God-focused, Holy Spirit-filled, and obedient to God, we take aim at living that life where our thoughts, speech, and actions line up with His will.

Many Christian pastors, speakers, and authors exhort us on the importance of conquering our minds in order to stay away from sin. By taking "dead aim" at God as our "target" and focusing on His precepts, we set up a trajectory that will help us say "No!" to sin, including relational recklessness.

We can also take "dead aim" against Satan by following the recipe for successful battle against our enemy. Our victory is found in Ephesians 6:10-20 where we learn to:

- Be strong in the Lord and in His mighty power
- Take a stand against the devil's schemes
- Know that our struggle is not against flesh and blood but against rulers, principalities, darkness, and evil
- Wear the full armor of God:
    - Helmet of Salvation
    - Breastplate of Righteousness
    - Belt of Truth
    - Shield of Faith (to extinguish Satan's flaming arrows)
    - Sword of the Spirit which is the Word of God

- - Feet fitted with the readiness that comes from the Gospel of Peace
- Be alert
- Pray always for all the saints

By following this "battle plan", we are able to gain the victory over the enemy. Our stand against Satan's tactics is strengthened when we focus on preparing for battle God's way with His protection. This allows us to take aim at the devil and win against sin.

These Scriptures are worth noting as well as memorizing:

> *Submit yourselves therefore to God. Resist the devil, and he will flee from you.* (James 4:7)

> *...this kind does not go out except by prayer and fasting.* (Matthew 17:21 (NKJV)

This last Scripture reminds us that some sin is so deeply entrenched and demonic that it requires prayer and fasting in order to break the stronghold. When we submit to God and receive His insight and guidance, we are able to see the enemy for who he is and resist his schemes. Satan has no choice but to flee when we stand in the authority that is ours in Christ Jesus.

Step Seven – Forgive Others

We know from various Scriptures that lack of forgiveness is a doorway into which Satan will enter to steal from you and bring defeat. If we refuse to forgive others, we are inviting trouble into our lives.

We need to ask God to place forgiveness in our heart and to help us have compassion for others and ourselves instead of hatred. It is certain that if you have been the victim of another person's sin, you need to forgive them. This is never easy. We never feel like forgiving others who have hurt us. Our flesh will tell us to take revenge rather than forgive others.

I *know* this is difficult, for I used to refuse to forgive people when they hurt me. I would brood for days, weeks, months, even years. I would go over and over the situation in my mind, thinking up better and nastier things that I should have said in the situation. The fights I had in my mind were both fantastic and insane.

As God healed my heart from the real culprit – feelings of rejection and low self-esteem – I became infinitely more compassionate with myself, and I dropped the perfectionism. Then, I could extend to others the same compassion, making it easier and easier for me to forgive others who hurt me. Of course, as we allow Jesus to sink really, really deep into our heart, we learn without doubt, as I did, that we belong to Him, and He guards our heart and mind, enabling us to extend forgiveness.

As a child of the King, nothing that anyone can say or do to you will ever cause God to stop loving you or wanting to be in a loving relationship with you. One thing I know beyond all doubt is that God never leaves us nor forsakes us like human beings do. Even when we sin, God still loves us with His extravagant love, although He, of course, desires that we stop sinning. When we turn away from sin permanently, we can again enjoy His Presence and fellowship. No person or thing or experience can remotely compare to the love of God.

Frankly, nothing that we chase after is worth ruining our fellowship with God and marring our worship of Him. If we would make a practice of the seven steps in this chapter, we will develop a strong relationship that will give us the strength to walk in His will. As a result, we will walk in the victory that is found in Jesus and fulfill the plans that God has for us, as is so clearly set out in one of my favorite passages of Scripture:

For I know the plans I have for you, declares the Lord, plans for welfare and not for evil, to give you a future and a hope.
~ Jeremiah 29:11

12

THE BIG PICTURE

*"If Christians around the world
were to suddenly renounce their personal agendas,
their life goals, and their aspirations,
and begin responding in radical obedience
to everything God showed them,
the world would be turned upside down.
How do we know?
Because that's what first century Christians did,
and the world is still talking about it."*[i]

Henry Blackaby

During the writing of this book, I worked through Henry Blackaby's landmark Bible study entitled *Experiencing God: Knowing and Doing the Will of God*. This was the first Bible study I had completed as a newly, minted believer in 2001. Interestingly, God brought this study to my attention again in 2016. It was a thrilling experience to work through this phenomenal study once more. I highly recommend it.

Presently, planet earth appears to have spun out of control. World events paint a sorry picture with grotesque terrorist activities occurring almost daily, unbridled violence, human trafficking, addictions, pandemics, destructive weather patterns, political corruption, etc., etc., etc. One could very easily lose all hope if we judged all things by what we see in the natural.

Satan illegally rules the earth having stolen that authority from Adam and Eve (through their own disobedience to God). Had Adam and Eve obeyed God and rejected the temptation offered by Satan in the Garden of Eden, they would have executed God's plan for them and for all of humanity – to have dominion over God's creation and be His ambassadors on the earth.

As a result of the transaction in the Garden of Eden, humans acquired a sin nature. Since that time, they have been hereditarily disposed to sinning and to indulging fleshly desires. The work of Christ on the cross, however, took that sin away and defeated Satan for all time. Still, our flesh continues to plague us and, in fact, is considered in the New Testament as a most powerful and influential enemy.[22]

Along with many other books, sermons, and teachings heard in many churches today, this book is concerned with ensuring that our walk as believers is unspoiled by sin and defeat. Yet, the primary objective of being clean of sin is not solely so that we can live in a comfortable, Christian bubble, safe and protected from the harshness of the world. The primary objective of declaring victory in Jesus and actually walking in victory free from the shackles of sin is so that we, as the collective body of believers, can be clean vessels through which God can work and complete His plans and purposes for this earth.

But what are His corporate purposes? The first two verses of the Lord's Prayer tell us plainly what those purposes are.

---

[22] See Romans 7:14 &18, Romans 8:1-7, Galatians 3:3, Galatians 5:13-21, Ephesians 2:3

> *"Our Father in heaven,*
> *hallowed be your name.*
> *Your kingdom come,*
> *your will be done,*
> *on earth as it is in heaven."*
> Matthew 6:9-10

Note the order in which our directives appear. After first glorifying and revering God, the very next thing we are to pray for is what I call the "Big Picture" – manifesting the Kingdom of God and the will of God on earth as it is done in Heaven. The question then becomes, what is the will of God? Next, how does the Kingdom of God manifest on earth, and what, if anything, is our part in that?

I must admit that, since I first completed Blackaby's study in 2001, I had slipped away from the understanding that I must look to see where God is active and working and join in with that activity. Instead, I found myself focused on what God could provide for me and would, most of the time, just inform God what I wanted to do for Him. Blackaby states that this thinking is backwards:

"What is God's will for my life?" is not the right question. I think the proper question is, "What is God's will?" Once I know God's will, then I can adjust my life to Him. In other words, what is it God is purposing to accomplish where I am? Once I know what God is doing, then I know what I need to do. The focus needs to be on God, not on my life!

When I want to learn how to know and do God's will, I can find no better model than Jesus' life. During His approximately 33 years on the earth, He perfectly completed every assignment the Father gave Him. He never failed to do the will of the Father, and He never sinned.[23]

After going through *Experiencing God* a second time, the impact of my backwards thinking was highlighted. I couldn't dictate my path to God. Instead, I needed to search out His will in everything, making His business my business.

---

[23] *Experiencing God* Bible Study (see Endnotes)

Using Scripture, Blackaby shows us seven truths[24] that we must keep in mind for living the Christian life.

- God is always at work;
- God pursues a love relationship with us;
- God invites us to become involved with Him in His work;
- God speaks to us through the Holy Spirit, the Bible, prayer, circumstances, and the church in order to reveal His purposes and ways;
- God's invitation then leads us to a crisis of belief that requires faith and action;
- If we decide to join God in His work, then we must make major adjustments in our lives; and
- Finally, we come to know God by experience as we obey Him and He accomplishes His work through us.

A great example of these truths at work is found in the life of Abraham. God spoke clearly to him, setting out His plans to create

---

[24] *Experiencing God* Bible Study (see Endnotes)

a great nation of people through Abraham's son Isaac. The plan, however, involved testing Abraham's character first with a directive to do what any right thinking person would consider heinous – he had to sacrifice his own son.

Abraham had to make a major adjustment in his life in order to join God in doing His will or "His activity". Because he loved and trusted God, Abraham interrupted his own plans and obeyed God's directive to ascend the mountain with his son, the intended sacrifice, in tow. How heartening it is to read that, even before he started up the mountain, Abraham knew without any doubt that God would spare Isaac and provide a lamb for the sacrifice:

After these things God tested Abraham and said to him, "Abraham!" And he said, "Here I am." He said, "Take your son, your only son Isaac, whom you love, and go to the land of Moriah, and offer him there as a burnt offering on one of the mountains of which I shall tell you." So Abraham rose early in the morning, saddled his donkey, and took two of his young men with him, and his son Isaac.

And he cut the wood for the burnt offering and arose and went to the place of which God had told him. On the third day Abraham lifted up his eyes and saw the place from afar. Then Abraham said to his young men, "Stay here with the donkey; I and the boy will go over there and worship and come again to you."
~ Genesis 22:1-5

By telling his servants that he and his son would return to them after they worshipped God at the altar, Abraham demonstrated that he remembered God's promise to him that, *through him and his promised seed,* God would create the nation of Israel. Why else would he tell his servants before ascending the mountain that "*I <u>and the boy</u> will...<u>come again</u> to you*"?

So what does all this have to do with the rest of this book?

Well, it's quite simple really. God clearly showed me after He rescued me out of sin that His plan was not merely to restore me from the wilderness in which I walked. His refining justice and merciful forgiveness of my sin was also for the greater purpose of me playing my part in establishing the will of God on earth as it is done in Heaven, or to put it in Blackaby's words, to "join God in His activity".

If I am caught up in sin and self-absorption, I am incapable of obeying His commands. As a result, I cannot join God's activity and the work that He is doing around me. I cannot participate in His work of establishing His will on earth as it is in Heaven. I am useless to Kingdom works and purposes.

Sinful conduct as a believer is thus a two-edged sword. Firstly, we mar our life-giving, loving relationship with God resulting in personal discontent and discomfort. We personally feel the effects of our sin against God through the separation it creates between the Father and us. Secondly, we bench ourselves from Team Jesus. We cannot contribute to His corporate objective of bringing His Kingdom to earth when sin affects the Team relationship. This includes making disciples of all nations, baptizing them in the name of the Father, the Son, and the Holy Spirit, and teaching them to obey all of God's commands.[25]

This is, of course, Satan's primary objective in bringing temptation to us: to encourage us to choose sin over obedience to God and to thereby disconnect us from God, rendering us useless to God and to His corporate purposes for all of mankind. Against this onslaught we must stand our ground and declare the truth that *"...he who is in you is greater than he who is in the world."* (1 John 4:4)

What a Savior we have in Christ Jesus!

Conceiving of us before the world even began, God made each of us with special gifts, talents, and abilities. He uniquely and lovingly designed both you and me. He desires a personal and loving relationship with His creation.

---

[25] See Matthew 28:19-20

However, He knows that we are weak and susceptible to temptations of the flesh. He knows that we will stumble like King David did as well as other regular, ordinary, and weak people in the Bible through whom God worked in mighty ways. In fact, the only people available to accomplish God's purposes on this earth are those who have sinned – imperfect people who don't have it all together and who have fallen into sin.

Still, God's objectives will prevail. The Bible is clear that Jesus will build His church and the gates of hell will not prevail against it![26] Furthermore, God is constantly at work around us and invites us in all our imperfections to join Him in that work, utilizing our unique gifts, talents, and abilities for His glory.

Satan wants to sabotage God's objectives here on earth. This is why he will bring every temptation possible to us in order to take us out. As I have experienced, there will be times when we stumble and fall into the

---

[26] Matthew 16:19

temptation that Satan is offering. Yet, when this happens, we must take heart! That need not be the end of the story! God is a redeeming God, ready to turn things around for the repentant heart.

Jesus was very clear when He told the disciples right before He ascended to Heaven that *all* authority of Heaven and earth had been given to Him. If we are going to take Jesus at His word, as we should, then we must know beyond all doubt that through Jesus, and by calling upon Him to help us, we can say "NO!" to sin, including relational recklessness.

On the cross of Calvary, Jesus accomplished two, critically important things:

1. Jesus vanquished Satan on the cross. He conquered death itself. He defeated Satan in the great, Heavenly battle. The Kingdom of God permanently beat the kingdom of Satan. Satan will never win against Jesus. Ever.

2. Jesus became sin on our behalf so that we could, upon our profession of faith in Christ, be restored to a right relationship with God. Jesus willingly endured the wrath of God on the cross, punishment that was meant for sinners, for us! If we confess our faith in Jesus, we are called sons and daughters of God[27]. Our original mandate is reinstated – that of being His ambassadors on earth and dominion-keepers of all His creation. We have the right to be inhabited by the Person of the Holy Spirit and are beneficiaries of His power, the very same power that raised Jesus from the grave!

Stop now and prayerfully consider these two realities. They are guaranteed because of who Jesus is based on His person and His character. Thus, you need to remind yourself of the fact that, as a saved believer, you are on the winning team!

If you have never trusted Jesus as your Lord and Savior, now is the time. Don't waste another minute of your life without Jesus.

---

[27] See 2 Corinthians 6:18

Repent of all your sin and humbly ask for His forgiveness for shutting Him out of your life. Ask Him to be your Lord and Savior, to come into your heart and change it. Then, get connected to a Bible-preaching church.

With Jesus at your side, you have all you need to successfully move forward in life. With His help, you can release all the sin habits that have held you in bondage and kept you in defeat. My life is a testimony to this fact and to the fact that, as a child of God, He never gives up on you.

It is my prayer that in the telling of my story, you will find encouragement and hope in the midst of whatever crisis you are going through. I pray that, if you are currently walking in sin, you look up and away from your circumstances to the God of your hope and salvation. Fall to your knees in repentance knowing, beyond a shadow of a doubt, that God sees you from afar and runs towards you as you return home, anxious to enfold you in His arms once again and forgive you of your sins. Allow yourself to be drawn into a deeper love relationship with the Father.

Furthermore, may this love relationship lead you to experience a rock solid trust in God the Father, the Son, and the Holy Spirit. As you trust Him, your faith will grow, leading you through the greatest adventure there is – a life lived securely in the middle of God's love and will. You *can* be certain in the guarantee that your sins are forgiven. You *can* walk in a newfound sense of hope and life. You can have this assurance and more because of God's incomprehensible Grace and Mercy that is yours because of Christ's work on the cross.

In addition, I pray that, through my story, you become aware of and understand the agenda of the enemy. The purposes of Satan are to destroy you and make you ineffective and useless within the Kingdom of God. It is critical that you discern all his tricks and wiles. As you learn to resist his tactics, always remember that greater is Jesus who resides in you than he (Satan) who resides in the world as we discovered in 1 John 4:4.

Finally, I pray that you honestly and prayerfully complete the work in this book. May my testimony encourage you to examine your own heart for sin habits and ways of thinking that are sabotaging your relationship with God and your faith walk. Walk through the reflections and exercises with the goal of excavating all the darkness that has taken up residence in your heart. Determine to surrender it all to Jesus, the only One who can remove all impediments, sorrows, pain, and sin. It's time to draw a line in the sand and say, "No more!" to relational recklessness.

I discovered that, with the knowledge and revelation of God imparted into my life and situation, I was without excuse. I could no longer relegate God to the background and ignore what I knew to be Truth. As uncomfortable and painful as it was, the freedom I now enjoy because of God's mighty, redeeming work in me is beyond what I could dream or imagine. This is the hope to which YOU are called as well!

No more excuses!

I leave you with one final passage of Scripture of encouragement for your journey:

There is therefore now no condemnation for those who are in Christ Jesus. For the law of the Spirit of life has set you free in Christ Jesus from the law of sin and death. For God has done what the law, weakened by the flesh, could not do. By sending his own Son in the likeness of sinful flesh and for sin, he condemned sin in the flesh, in order that the righteous requirement of the law might be fulfilled in us, who walk not according to the flesh but according to the Spirit.

...*in all these things we are more than conquerors through him who loved us.* [28]
~ Romans 8:1-4, 37

There is hope. There is healing. There is redemption. IN JESUS, you *can* and *will* be victorious!

Be blessed!

---

[28] Emphasis mine

ABOUT THE AUTHOR

Leslie J. Smith was born in Galt, Ontario, and raised in London, Ontario. Before attending Windsor Law at the University of Windsor, Leslie obtained a degree in Early Childhood Education from Ryerson Polytechnical Institute (now Ryerson University).

Leslie was called to the Bar in Ontario in 1988. When she opened her own practice in 1996, in Oakville, Ontario, Leslie began her work as an Employment Lawyer and was the author of the popular 'Legal Ease' column for the Burlington Post Newspaper from 1997-2014. Her years of experience in the area of employment as it relates to the law led her to publish her first book, *Legal Ease—Essential Legal Strategies to Protect Canadian Non-Union Employees*, published in 2014. (To purchase this excellent resource book, go to www.legaleasecanada.com.) She's also a Mediator.

An accomplished speaker and presenter, Leslie is passionate about her work and her testimony. With a no-nonsense approach, she tells it like it is while encouraging her audiences to be honest, do what is right, and make the changes necessary to be successful and live their best life. She is 100% sold out for God.

In sharing her personal story, Leslie has made herself vulnerable for the sake of the Kingdom. Seeing the bigger picture, she knows that her experiences – and what she learned from them – can be worked together for God's Glory. Her deepest desire is that the readers of *Without Excuse—Saying "No!" to Relational Recklessness* will find their way back to right relationship with God. In her no-nonsense way, she aims to expose the enemy – the ultimate liar – and destroy his plans so that the Kingdom of God can be established on earth as it is in Heaven.

Leslie is the proud mother of three adult children and currently lives in Oakville, Ontario. When she is not working, Leslie enjoys reading, hiking, camping, and being outdoors.

ENDNOTES

[i] *Experiencing God: Knowing and Doing the Will of God.* Published by LifeWay Press, © 2007 Henry Blackaby, Richard Blackaby, and Claude King. Reprinted 2015. Duplicated and used by permission.

Made in the USA
Middletown, DE
11 September 2017